A
Smoother
Journey

A
Smoother
Journey

by
Simon Schrock

New Leaf Press

First printing: April 1994
Second printing: February 1995

ISBN: 0-89221-267-5
Library of Congress Catalog: 94-67321

All Scripture quotations are from the King James Version of the Bible, unless otherwise indicated.

Cover photo by: J & J Tiner Photographs

Dedication

To the late Cliff Dudley, in appreciation for his fellowship in Christ, his concern for good reading, and for the publication of my books;

And to his wife, Harriett, for her warm Christian spirit and her faithfulness in living the life of a widow;

And to their children, Tim and Becky, for carrying on the work of the publishing company.

A special thanks to David (D.J.) King for his diligent typing of the manuscript.

Introduction

Life is a journey! You travel this journey from the time of your birth until your exit at death. It is a journey with millions of other people. In your travels others bump you, and you bump others. It is indeed a journey with numerous bumps and collisions.

For many, the journey is difficult traveling alongside of others. For some, it seems impossible. And a few face the challenge to make it an extra fruitful journey that blesses the lives of fellow travelers.

This journey is an experience with many people. From the moment of your birth until your burial, people are involved. Someone cared for the infant you. As your journey continues, many others contribute to your life. And you will have countless opportunities to contribute to others. This is called relationships.

The damage from the bumps along the journey are somewhat determined by the quality of your relationships. This also determines the richness of your contributions.

There are three things you can do with relationships. I grew up on a farm where I was soon introduced to the "bearings" in the machines. Bearings and relationships have something in common. If the bearing is oiled, the machine runs smoothly for a long time. If sand gets into the bearing, it quickly breaks down. If nothing is done — no oil, no sand — it eventually runs dry, squeaks, and burns out.

So it is in a relationship. You have three choices. You can do nothing and watch it eventually diminish. You can drop in some sand and hear the death crunch. Or you can keep it oiled and nurture it.

With God, your relationship with Him is his highest priority. His second priority is for you to have a good relationship with your fellow travelers. I'm working at making these priorities a part of my walk of life. In the process, this book is sharing some insights from God's Word on keeping oil in the relationship bearings. It is challenging, sometimes painful, and takes deliberate effort. Join me in working for *A Smoother Journey* through the relationships of life.

— Simon Schrock

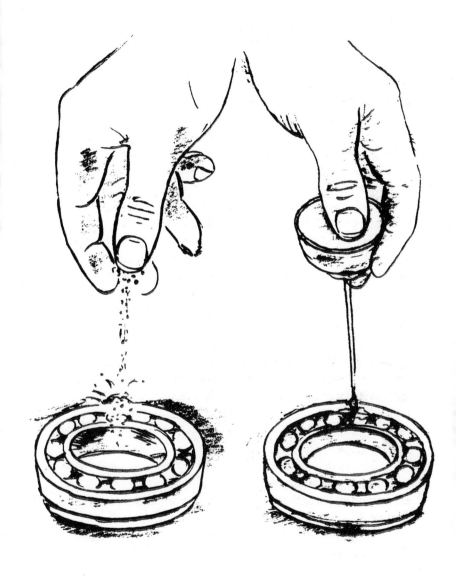

Illustration by Mac Olsen

Contents

1. Stop and Reflect 11

2. Check Your Priorities 19

3. Wrong Comes Naturally 29

4. The Holy Limp 37

5. Love Covers, Hatred Cancels 47

6. Sin Separates 55

7. Shock Absorbers and Jesus 63

8. Solemnly Reprove — But How? 71

9. Making Wrongs Right 85

10. Oil of Forgiveness 95

11. Me People — We People 113

12. The Beauty of Accountability 123

13. Harmony in the Workplace 135

14. Authority and Our Relationships with Others 147

15. It Could Mean Suffering! 155

16. Have a Friend, Be a Friend 165

17. Making Needed Changes 173

Chapter 1

Stop and Reflect

Stop! Stop your journey of life! Turn around and look at the road you have just traveled. Are there broken, shattered friendships reminding you of past failures? Have you bumped someone off and left them lying by the road side? Have you inflicted hurts that have crippled your fellow travelers and left them disabled and waiting for help?

I was driving a van one dark night on a North Carolina highway. The interior light was on while my associate and I were trying to find our way on this unfamiliar road. In what seemed like a split second, our eyes caught a glimpse of a hitchhiker flash by the right hand side of our vehicle, and simultaneously there was a thump as the right wheel hit an object.

My heart sank! I knew I had hit someone. As we turned around to go back, I could envision a body splattered over the road. With a sick feeling we approached the object on the highway. I thought I had killed a child. Not until we were closer to the object did we discover it was a bag of clothes instead of a person. The hitchhiker had run away, leaving his clothes scattered on the highway. As I relive the incident, my emotions shrink and cringe at the thought of killing a person.

Leave this frightening ride on the highway and think about the journey of life. In our trip of life, we bump others off the road, and leave them lying there to hurt and die. We practice hit-and-run driving. I am not referring to physical bodies, but to relationships. I am speaking of relationship casualties.

Look at the roadway you have traveled. Reflect on your past travels. Does your driving cause travelers to go far to the side of the road? Do you occasionally feel a thud? Do you swing out to pass, and bump others off the road? Are there casualties lying along the road you have traveled? Are there wounded waiting for help?

Stop and reflect! Look back in your journey of life. How many dead relationships lie beside your path from head-on collisions? How many wounded and crippled are lying there with heart pain? Is there someone with a cast or a bandage on a broken spirit or wounded emotions? Is there someone with deep stomach pains or ulcers as a result of your pickled tongue?

Is someone applying a heating pad in their depression, because of having too much draft from your cold shoulder? Is your relationship road scattered with casualties and wounded friendships?

What about the person with whom you disputed, and won the argument, but now resent?

What about that friend who attempted to point out a fault, so you just wrote him off?

What about the person who was blessed just a little more in temporal things than you? Did jealousy set in and freeze your friendly smile?

What about the person you could not manage to control, so you just slowly nudged him or her outside of your social circle?

In many of my travels I hear of people's hurts, frustrations, and angers because of strained relationships. That is the discussion at lunch tables across the land. That is the discussion in airliners flying thousands of feet above the earth, in small groups after the church business meeting, in the boss's office. It is the conversation piece after the children are in bed. Pastors hear these stories constantly. People everywhere are hurting because of strained and broken relationships.

I know a father and a son who do not communicate with each other. The son parted ways with his parents, leaving them crushed, bruised, and wounded. The father, mother, and son are all emotionally crippled with deep spiritual struggles.

Throughout the Church there are fathers and sons who are not communicating, and who do not get along. They are emotional enemies! Many sons take a last look at their father in the coffin, and must live the rest of their lives with the memories of a bad relationship.

An aging mother-in-law cries with pain as she tells of the wounds and hurts of a strained in-law relationship. The in-law jokes we hear are not jokes at all, they are the result of deep emotional wounds.

An old man spends the last days of his life in grief and sorrow, because of the cold rejection of family members.

I know husbands and wives who went to the marriage altar like two lovebirds, but today they speak to each other with bitterness, resentment, and antagonism. Wives may pout for days because of disappointments, while husbands stay away from home in anger. Too often couples may choose divorce, a thing God hates, rather than assume responsibility for their own wrong.

People with resentments will spend money, time, and energy to avoid those with whom they are at odds. They will not give a dime to express love and kindness toward their emotional enemies, but will spend hundreds of dollars to avoid them.

I know a woman who is an emotional wreck, and simply cannot enjoy a victorious Christian life. She was emotionally inflicted with a bruise that will not go away. She was wronged in her young life, and that wrong was never made right. Occasionally she manages to get to her feet and walk, then the pain strikes, the wound is torn open, and she struggles by the wayside.

There are others who spend their days walking under clouds of depression because of strained and broken relationships. These clouds leave them feeling hated and rejected. Their clouds greet them at daybreak, and hover over them everywhere they go.

I know two neighbors who were close friends. There was social and family interaction, sharing and helping each other. Then the picture changed. Instead of helping each other, it is now competition, cold shouldering, faultfinding, working against each other, and trying to make life miserable for the other. These two people are relationship casualties in each other's lives. Both of them suffer and hurt from hardships life brings on. How wonderful if they could enjoy coffee together, pray, share, and cry together. How beautiful it would be if they could comfort one another. Instead, they are thorns in each other's flesh.

There are two brothers who are out of fellowship with each other. Both of them anticipate spending eternity with their Redeemer. I have listened to hours of charges leveled by one against the other. Life goes on, but they refuse to be reconciled.

Bob and Phil are members of two Bible-believing churches. They have broken fellowship over a business deal.

There are pastors who walk out and leave the church. Others go and take part of the congregation with them. Still others fall into moral sin and are defeated. Often the long roots can be traced to relationship problems in the church.

These few illustrations have taken place within the Church. And I ask, is this the will of God? Must life be this way? Is there a better way that most believers have failed to practice?

When you find this kind of behavior among unbelievers, it is understandable. When you find it among believers, it is unacceptable.

The evening sun had just gone behind the trees and darkness was coming on. I was coming home from a bike ride and as I approached the Choice Books building, I noticed a small gathering of young people in the parking lot. When I got there, two of them rolled over on the grass in what one bystander referred to as a good "all-American fight." I discovered it was indeed a fight. It had something to do with a girlfriend. The larger of the two boys seemed to have a distinct advantage, and appeared to be unmerciful to the smaller one under him. The smaller boy's brother picked up a 2 x 4 laying nearby, and struck the fellow on top with a heavy blow. He rolled over on the grass with pain. My intervention stopped further violence, and the disgruntled group disbanded.

That is how some people express themselves when things do not go their way. That is the natural, inborn, inherited way of settling or expressing displeasure.

Is this God's way of handling conflict? What might happen if these neighbor boys do not properly resolve their dispute?

Could the fight lead to lifelong enemies? Or a murder? It has all the potential of becoming worse, and just may be a bigger miracle if it does not.

Two sisters-in-law lived across the road from each other. Their relationship deteriorated over the years. They were not on loving or speaking terms. One day the home of one of these ladies caught fire. She hurried across the road to her sister-in-law's home to call the fire department. Her angry, resentful sister-in-law did not permit her to use the phone. She had to go to another neighbor's home further away. As a result, she lost her home.

Sin in relationships is never satisfied. Unresolved and unforgiven anger and resentment can never have their hunger filled. It requires yet another act of animosity, yet another try at revenge and getting even.

Ezekiel points out that Israel went so far as shocking the Philistines with their greed and lewd conduct. After they went into the depth of sin and prostitution, the Prophet said, ". . . and even after that, you still were not satisfied. Then you increased your promiscuity to include Babylonia, a land of merchants, but even with this you were not satisfied" (Ezek. 16:28-29;NIV).

Sin Never Satisfies

It always demands yet another step of revenge or anger.

Jesus said, "You have heard that it was said to the people long ago, 'Do not murder, and anyone who murders will be subject to judgment.' But I tell you that anyone who is angry with his brother will be subject to judgment . . ." (Matt. 5:21-22;NIV).

The Bible says, "Whosoever hateth his brother is a murderer: and ye know that no murderer hath eternal life abiding in him" (1 John 3:15).

Sin at any level demands yet another act of revenge. Early one November morning, a Fairfax County man was gunned down after he stepped out of his pickup truck to inspect possible damage from a minor rear-end collision. As the driver stepped out of the truck to inspect the damage, a gunman fired 20 to 30 shots at the victim. The assailant apparently blamed the victim for something that happened 12 years ago, and harbored a grudge that festered over the years.

Believers would seldom resort to physical murder, however, bad relationships have other consequences.

A number of years ago, a man in New York made the mistake of drinking some clam chowder that was so hot it burned his esophagus, doing permanent damage that made it impossible for him to swallow. The only solution his doctors could devise was to pull out a portion of his stomach lining so'that he could put food directly into his stomach. It does not sound like a very tasty way to eat, but one side benefit was that his doctors had the opportunity of observing how his emotions affected his digestion.

One fact quickly became apparent. Nothing was more stressful than his relationship with people. Anger, resentment, or bitterness would raise the acid level abruptly, and cause his stomach lining to swell. As they watched, his stomach told the story of a friendship gone astray. The stomach wall turned red, began to bleed, and developed an ulcer. In other words, that churning feeling in your stomach when a friendship goes astray is not just a feeling. Bad friendships destroy good stomachs.[1]

Three Things You Can Do

There are basically three things you can do with your friendships. One, follow the teachings of Scripture, and work on building a good, ongoing relationship that is rewarding for the other person and for yourself.

A second choice you have is to follow a pattern that destroys relationships. That can easily be done by doing whatever your selfish inclination desires.

The third option is to do absolutely nothing. Doing nothing, I can assure you, will cause the relationship to die.

Let me illustrate. Consider the ball bearing on your car axle. That bearing will last a long time if there is proper lubrication. Grease on a bearing will make it run smoother and last much longer. The oil of biblical principles, divine love, of doing what is right, will maintain a smooth, enjoyable relationship. Proverbs gives us an abundance of oil for relationships. "A patient man calms a quarrel" (Prov. 15:18;NIV).

If you drop sand into the bearing, it will be ruined in a short time, sometimes instantly. The sand of our self-will principles will destroy a relationship in short order.

The third option, to do absolutely nothing, no sand, nor oil, just nothing, will destroy the bearing. It will soon run dry and be ruined. So it is in relationships. To just back out and do nothing will kill it dead. It takes longer than sand in a bearing, but is just as deadly.

An example of what sand and oil will do can be seen in the life of Jacob and his sons. Jacob sanded the relationship with his older sons by showing favoritism to his younger son, Joseph. They reacted, and *chose* to follow the self-will principles in relationships. They applied the sinful, destructive sands of hatred and more hatred, followed by envy. With hatred and envy burning in their hearts, they conspired to kill. They finally chose a lesser offense — one that is very popular today. They decided that they needed more room, and just had to get away from Joseph for a while. That would solve the relationship problem. They gave themselves room, all right.

While Joseph was drawing closer to God they were burdened with the guilt of their actions, lies, and cover-up. For 20 years they suffered because of relationship casualties.

The sand of hatred in their relationship alienated Joseph from his brethren. It separated father and son, and broke the father's heart.

Joseph is an example of one who applied the oil of Godly principles.

Joseph applied the oil of being present with his brothers in their time of extreme relationship tensions.

He applied the oil of a broken spirit before them.

He applied the oil of tears and sorrow.

He applied the oil of speaking the truth in love, and said, "I am Joseph."

He applied the oil of inviting them to come near, to come to him, to touch and forgive.

He gave them comfort, acceptance, and forgiveness.

He gave the oil of a kiss to his brothers, he embraced, and let the healing oil of tears flow.

Following this, the oil of communication began to flow freely.

Joseph's proper response to these circumstances brought another tremendous reward. Joseph and his father were reunited. They embraced, and Joseph wept a long time.

Can't you just feel the release of guilt and tension being washed away with these tears? And then his father said, ". . . Now I am ready to die, since I have seen for myself that you are still alive" (Gen. 46:30;NIV).

We live in a world with more than five billion other people, and in a country with 236 million individuals. I live in a county with over 700,000 people. I must learn to get along, especially if I mix with them in rush-hour traffic. I live, work, and drive closely with others. I constantly relate to others. God wants me to apply oil in my relationships. It starts with those closest to me.

Your choices are simply these:

You can apply oil and have a good relationship.

You can pour sand, and hurt and destroy relationships and people.

You can do nothing, and let relationships slowly die like a starving person. Death may take time, but it is sure.

God asks and expects believers to apply oil in their relationships. They are to apply a healing balm in the same spirit as His servant Joseph did. That oil heals and preserves relationships.

Chapter 2

Check Your Priorities

Look ahead! The highway of life lies before you. Will you continue to bump others off to the side, and leave them wounded and dying while you do a hit and run? How many of those people on the road ahead of you will become relationship casualties? How many will you bump off?

It depends! It depends on what you do with an important relationship principle. For those who truly grasp this principle, it will revolutionize their lifestyle. They will become safe and pleasant travelers on the journey of life. On the other hand, those who miss this principle will continue to look back and see wounded and dying relationships along their journey.

This is a very important foundational principle to good relationships. If you miss this, and do not make it a part of your life, you will not experience satisfaction and fulfillment in relationships.

Priority #1

Loving God and walking with Him is to be the highest priority in our life. It is to be priority number one in our relationships.

God created man and woman to have fellowship and a meaningful relationship with himself. This relationship was broken by sin. Humanity became a relationship casualty. However;

God sent His Son, Jesus Christ, to the earth, to go to the Cross, hang there in midday, and to bear the punishment for our sins. Jesus came to bring us together again in a restored relationship with God, and with each other.

In response, God commands, "And thou shalt love the Lord thy God with all thine heart, and with all thy soul, and with all thy might" (Deut. 6:5). When we truly grasp that it is God's command that our first priority must always be to love and obey Him, that will develop and mold our way of life into one that glorifies Him.

Priority #2

The church leaders call for a business meeting with the membership. The pastor presents the dire need for more support for the school fund. This is to be high on our priority list. God wants us to give.

You receive a flyer in the mail. It has pictures of little children that look like skin and bones with their stomachs bulging from improper nutrition and starvation. There is an urgent plea to your emotions to move you to compassion and give. Send your check now! The fact is, Jesus wants us to give.

Is this what God intends to be our second priority?

Let us go to the Scriptures to determine.

God gave Israel these instructions. "Thou shalt not avenge, nor bear any grudge against the children of thy people, but thou shalt love thy neighbour as thyself: I am the Lord" (Lev. 19:18).

Paul referred to this law when he wrote of Christian liberty in Christ. "For all the law is fulfilled in one word, even in this; Thou shalt love thy neighbour as thyself" (Gal. 5:14).

James draws attention to the royal law. "If ye fulfil the royal law according to the scripture, Thou shalt love thy neighbour as thyself, ye do well: But if ye have respect to persons, ye commit sin, and are convinced of the law as transgressors" (James 2:8-9).

Jesus leaves no question as to what God's priorities are. "Jesus said unto him, Thou shalt love the Lord thy God with all thy heart, and with all thy soul, and with all thy mind. This is the first and great commandment. And the second is like unto it, Thou shalt love thy neighbour as thyself. On these two commandments hang all the law and the prophets" (Matt. 22:37-40).

Jesus, along with all Scripture, makes it clear that the believers' second priority is people and relationships.

Let's continue in the Scripture to see how high a priority God places on good relationships.

"If it be possible, as much as lieth in you, live peaceably with all men" (Rom. 12:18).

"Owe no man any thing, but to love one another: for he that loveth another hath fulfilled the law. For this, Thou shalt not commit adultery, Thou shalt not kill, Thou shalt not steal, Thou shalt not bear false witness, Thou shalt not covet; and if there be any other commandment, it is briefly comprehended in this saying, namely, Thou shalt love thy neighbour as thyself. Love worketh no ill to his neighbour: therefore love is the fulfilling of the law" (Rom. 13:8-10).

"Let us therefore follow after the things which make for peace, and things wherewith one may edify another" (Rom. 14:19).

"We then that are strong ought to bear the infirmities of the weak, and not to please ourselves. Let every one of us please his neighbour for his good to edification. For even Christ pleased not himself; but, as it is written, The reproaches of them that reproached thee fell on me" (Rom. 15:1-3).

"Salt is good: but if the salt have lost his saltness, wherewith will ye season it? Have salt in yourselves, and have peace one with another" (Mark 9:50).

"Flee also youthful lusts: but follow righteousness, faith, charity, peace, with them that call on the Lord out of a pure heart" (2 Tim. 2:22).

"Follow peace with all men, and holiness, without which no man shall see the Lord" (Heb. 12:14).

Paul makes it a priority to live with a free conscience before God and man. "And herein do I exercise myself, to have always a conscience void of offense toward God, and toward men" (Acts 24:16).

The church funds need money. Children are starving. Are these things God's second priorities? Do these things come next to loving God? Let's see what Jesus said about it! "Therefore if thou bring thy gift to the altar, and there rememberest that thy brother hath ought against thee; Leave there thy gift before the altar, and go thy way; first be reconciled to thy brother, and then come and offer thy gift" (Matt. 5:23-24).

Jesus set the record straight! Right relationships take priority over anything else in this life. God wants your money. God wants you to help starving children. But more important than that, He wants you to have good relationships.

God knows that when good relationships are placed in proper perspective in your life, you will then, out of a heart of love, reach for your checkbook, and joyfully give to the Church and other worthy projects.

Here is the principle in good relationships. God places good relationships as number two on His priority list for believers. He wants you to make that number two in your priorities. If you do not have good relationships with others, and are not loving them as yourself, you are out of tune with God.

I wonder if we tend to look at this second commandment as some kind of duty or ritual we perform several times a month, or a shifting of our voice to the "nice" gear about twice a week. But no, my friend, it is not a duty we perform, or a ritual we go through, or a nice show we put on.

It is a way of life!

It is a pattern we practice and follow in living!

It is a principle we follow in decision making!

When God is priority number one, and relationships are number two, then the questions are: Does it please God, and how does it affect my relationships with people around me? This is not compatible with the all-American attitude that I am my own person, free to pursue my own interests, make a name for myself, and at liberty to do what I want when I choose to, regardless of how it affects my neighbor. James Hilt wrote, "Our culture glorifies independence, self-sufficiency, and toughness."[1] The Scriptures direct us to a better way.

How do we then translate priority number two into our daily lives?

Assume there is a family disposal sale. You and your sister both want the old grandfather clock. You know you have the financial means to buy the clock. Your sister has a large family, and has had some large medical bills, and as a result, cannot outbid you. So it is yours for the taking! Right?

If relationships are priority, the question will not be whether you can outbid your sister, but what will it do to your relationship?

You might purchase the clock, but lose the relationship. It may well be that the clock will strike out painful reminders every hour, that you have a clock and a hurting sister. Your children may ask, "Why doesn't Aunt Mary speak freely with us anymore?" You both wanted the old clock, but only one could actually have it. An earthly, perishable thing has destroyed your open relationship with your sister's family.

You may *manipulate* to stay in control of the entire situation, but in the process drive people away.

You might *win* the argument, but lose the friendship.

You may be able to *monopolize* the conversation, but in the process kill a relationship.

When relationships are our priority, the first questions asked are not "How much money? What is in it for me? What do I gain?" Rather, "What does it do to our relationship?"

Why Must Relationships Be Priority?

First, the quality of your life depends on your relationships. When relationships are not in place, everything else is out of place. There is nothing that can take its place. Its dark cloud hangs over you, and controls you wherever you go. Go to work, it meets you there. Go to the mountains, it follows you there. Go to see Aunt Lizzie, and it shows up there. It controls your attitudes and actions with others, and even your response as you walk past the family dog.

"Better a meal of vegetables where there is love than a fattened calf with hatred" (Prov. 15:17;NIV).

Joe and Ruth Ann can afford the finest dining, eat at the most expensive restaurants, and make their friends jealous with their frequent vacations around the world. But they do not know what it is to simply enjoy a hamburger together. They can discuss the quality of food and the service they are given, but they really cannot communicate with each other. Take away the triviality of those fine napkins, and there is nothing left to say. Your ability to enjoy life does not depend on being able to see the world and eating T-bone. It depends on the quality of your relationships. When relationships are good, the world looks better, even from your dining room window. Hamburgers or T-bone take on new flavor.

Secondly, it shapes your beliefs and values. Brad's parents were sincere Bible-believing Christians. They taught their son right from wrong. They were committed to teaching Brad the way he should go. He was taught the doctrine of Scripture, and the right things about God. But he did not enjoy a good family relationship.

One day Brad left home. He left the Church and the doctrines of the Bible that he had been taught. He flaunted the ways of the world before his parents. His actions hurt them deeply.

Why did Brad do this? Did he change his position on theology? No, in fact, he never formed much of a position for himself. He left home because of strained relationships. *Then he adjusted his belief to fit the broken relationship.*

We are a mobile people. We spend time and money moving to the right place, going from one relationship to another, one church to another, often leaving sound doctrine for false teaching. Is it because we have become enlightened on Scripture? Usually not! I am discovering that we change our position on scriptural teaching more often as a result of a strained relationship than any other reason.

The person who changes his position on divorce and remarriage does so as a result of a broken relationship.

Good relationships are essential for maintaining sound doctrine. The religious scandals that have hung over the community of believers are deeply rooted in poor relationships and unscriptural responses.

A third reason is that everybody needs a friend. It is significant to notice how friendship played an important role in the lives of the men of God in Scripture.

Moses had Aaron and Joshua to support him.

David had loyal friends, most notably Jonathan.

Daniel lived a remarkable life of faith, surrounded by three friends.

Jesus himself interwove His life with twelve men, of whom three were especially close, and John was the closest of the three.

Paul constantly associated with an intimate circle of friends, and as he faced death at Nero's hand, he urged Timothy to "Do your best to come to me quickly . . . . Only Luke is with me . . ." (2 Tim. 4:9-11;NIV).

Gary Inrig wrote, "The fact that such heroes of faith needed others underlines the inescapable need we all have to establish solid and satisfying friendships that not only meet our needs, but equip us to meet the needs of others as well."[2]

The writer of the apocryphal book spoke the truth when he wrote, "A faithful friend is a strong shelter; the man who has found one has found a treasure. There is no substitute for a friend, and there is no way to measure his value."

The fourth aspect is here today, maybe not tomorrow. Today relationships are here; tomorrow they may not be. Today I can talk with you, a living, breathing, warm person. Tomorrow it may not be so. Today I can shake your warm hand, look into your eyes, and say "God bless you." You can smile back. Tomorrow you or I may be cold and lifeless — gone on to our eternal destiny.

Believe me, I know. I stood and watched my 16-year-old brother take his last breath when I was about 21.

I hurried to my sister-in-law and her husband's car to discover what was wrong with my wife, and found her unconscious. And then . . . on a Friday evening about 5 p.m., the doctor told me it was over. A young 26-year-old man could only touch a cold body.

In February of 1981, my friends were waiting for me to return home to tell me that my father had died very suddenly. He and Mother were eating supper. He asked for applesauce, and suddenly dropped over dead. Never again would my father communicate with my mother or me.

In September 1977, Faith Christian Fellowship held a dedication service for the new church building. The congregation was forming, and soon her leaders would be called from the congregation. I had sensed that this might be the time God would call me to the ministry. If God chose to call me at that time, I anticipated working with the congregation, and especially our elder church father, Willie Byler.

After the dedication service, Willie and his wife left for a vacation. We said our goodbyes and blessings, and they left. The next time I saw his body, it was cold and lifeless.

Yes, I was ordained to the ministry, but the privilege of having Willie's counsel was gone.

Today you can eat a cookie and drink coffee with a friend. Today you can squeeze your son's hand. Today you can say "I love you" to your spouse, and laugh, cry, and pray together.

What happens if death takes a loved one, and you were filled with animosity toward that person? Of course, you can experience God's forgiveness, but fellowship with that individual cannot be restored.

What happens if you die suddenly, and you were filled with animosity, hatred, and bitterness? Will God's grace wipe everything away? Perhaps . . . but do not be presumptuous about the grace of God.

Examples of Getting Priorities in the Right Place

Harold resented his father. He managed to keep his visits brief and avoid confrontation. When his father was fighting his final battle with cancer, Harold went to visit him. "Dad," he said, "I really feel for what has happened to you. It has helped me look at the ways I have kept my distance, and to feel I really love you." As he leaned over to give his dad a hug, he felt his father's shoulders and arms grow tense.

Harold felt the resentment return, and he was ready to walk out. Then he thought again. He realized the hug was for his benefit as well as his father's.

Harold's father was dying. Restoring the relationship became a priority for him. He visited his father. He hugged him, and told him, "I love you." About the two hundredth time, his father spontaneously said out loud, for the first time Harold could ever recall, "I love you." Harold gained inner peace. His relationship with others took on a new dimension.

I observed my parents express a living demonstration of putting relationships into proper perspective. Years ago when I was home for a visit, my brother and I were in the barn talking. He related a story to me that built deep respect in me for my parents.

My father had borrowed money to buy the home farm from a local believer, and a local lady in town. Then the Depression hit, and he could not continue paying the interest payments. So when the interest came due, the church brother came, walked down the row of cows, picked out the best (perhaps my brother's favorite), and led her away as payment for the interest. He needed that money about as much as I need a Leer jet. The lady from town (I do not know what her Christian commitment was) kept my father from going under. She said she knew he would pay when he could. She was patient and long-suffering.

As I relive that story, I recall seeing this church brother sitting at my parents' table, and enjoying dinner. The way my parents invited this man and his wife to dinner was a demonstration to me of what it means to have relationships in priority.

When God's priorities become your priorities, then you will reach for the oil instead of sand. You will be moved to apply the oil of healing rather than simply doing nothing.

Chapter 3

Wrong Comes Naturally

On a cold winter day in December 1936 a baby boy was born in Garret County, Maryland. His brothers were in the barn skinning an opossum when the announcement came that a baby was born. Having caught an opossum was a major achievement for them. The excitement of skinning their catch and having a fur business was in their system. The announcement of a baby brother was an intrusion into their own self-interest. Hindsight seems to indicate that they were more excited about catching an opossum than having a new baby brother.

Nevertheless, when this baby was born, he came into the world with a standard equipment package that all babies have. He was equipped with the package of original sin.

I was that baby, born while my brothers were engrossed with their opossum skinning. I am sure that once they left their hobby and saw their new brother, it was not long until they learned that he also had an interest of his own. The original sin package soon revealed itself as I cried and screamed to express my self-interest.

This original sin has put into the blood stream of each human a *burning passion to exalt and elevate* himself. Very soon after he takes his first breath, he begins to scream for what he wants, when he wants it, and he expects someone to provide it for him.

This original sin is a killer of relationships. It is what broke the relationship of the first man and woman with their God. It then caused extreme strain in their relationship with each other. They did not even complete their conversation with God before Adam blamed Eve for the problem. Guess how Eve must have resented Adam for blaming her.

All of humanity that followed Adam and Eve was born with a broken relationship, and with the ingredients for destroying relationships with their fellow humans. Cain, the first man born on this earth, became angry with his brother and murdered him. Born into this man was the natural inclination to automatically, without effort on his own, do the wrong things that destroyed his relationships. His anger and fighting spirit needed no self-starter or starting fluid. It needed no coaxing. *It was inborn, ready to ignite and explode. And it did!* Consequently, the relationship was destroyed for life.

This same destructive ingredient is born into all of us. We are filled with destructive poison. As a deadly cobra, by its very nature, strikes to inflict its venom into the victim, so the very nature of humanity is filled with poison, coiled and ready to strike. We are like time bombs ready to explode. *Striking and exploding comes naturally and needs no coaxing.*

Here is a principle we must grasp and understand if we want to have good relationships: The actions and attitudes that destroy relationships with God and others come naturally. They come to us without any conscious effort on our part. It is in our blood, and flows freely through our whole system. Your *tongue* is ready to lash out and speak evil. Your *face* is ready to frown with anger, your *hands* are ready to point at others, and your *feet* are ready to walk away and pout. The things that destroy relationships flow naturally. Dale E. Galloway gives us this reminder, "Man's inability to get along with his fellow man is a constant threat to the structure of our civilization. MAN DESPERATELY NEEDS HELP!"[1]

Civilization is under the threat of destruction as the time bombs lay waiting to explode within ourselves. In order to help us understand ourselves, let the Scripture speak to our need and condition. Jeremiah gives us the painful truth of what is in our heart. He said, "The heart is deceitful above all things, and desperately wicked: who can know it?" (Jer. 17:9). "Who can understand the human heart? There is nothing else so deceitful: it is too sick to be healed" (Jer. 17:9;TEV).

Somehow we have the idea we are pretty good with a few flaws now and then. Jeremiah saw it differently.

Oswald Chambers wrote, "Most of us have no ear for anything but ourselves, anything that is not me we cannot hear."[2]

In our hearts is implanted the wicked and deceitful ingredient that looks out for ME as Cain did when he murdered his brother. The prophet points out to us that there is no good thing in our hearts that is pressing to express itself. Our heart is not naturally endowed and filled with love, kindness, and righteousness. With a wicked heart comes a tongue that expresses itself and spews out its destroying poison.

"Even so the tongue is a little member, and boasteth great things. Behold, how great a matter a little fire kindleth! And the tongue is a fire, a world of iniquity: so is the tongue among our members, that it defileth the whole body, and setteth on fire the course of nature; and it is set on fire of hell. For every kind of beasts, and of birds, and of serpents, and of things in the sea, is tamed, and hath been tamed of mankind: But the tongue can no man tame; it is an unruly evil, full of deadly poison" (James 3:5-8).

This Scripture, penned for us by James, establishes the principle that destructive behavior comes naturally. Just open your mouth and out it comes. I do not have to go into my study, get on my knees, and persevere in prayer that evil attitudes will enter my heart and flow from the tip of my tongue. I do not have to entreat God for evil words to say about another. I do not have to prayerfully seek for anger to set itself aflame in my heart. It is all there, fighting against the holding restraint of the Holy Spirit.

It was the natural instinct in Joseph's brothers that responded to his presence with hatred. It was the natural flow of words that agreed to put him in a pit, and then sell him to the Ishmaelites.

It was the natural instinct in the people at the church

business meeting that went from words to "chairs . . . in the air as . . . brothers and sisters were hurling them at each other."[3]

It is our natural instinct to hurl bitter words, to bump into each other with ice cold shoulders, and to turn a bitter back.

Another Scripture that speaks specifically of our condition is Paul's writings to the Romans.

"What then? are we better than they? No, in no wise: for we have before proved both Jews and Gentiles, that they are all under sin; As it is written, There is none righteous, no, not one: There is none that understandeth, there is none that seeketh after God. They are all gone out of the way, they are together become unprofitable; there is none that doeth good, no, not one. Their throat is an open sepulchre; with their tongues they have used deceit; the poison of asps is under their lips: Whose mouth is full of cursing and bitterness: Their feet are swift to shed blood: Destruction and misery are in their ways: And the way of peace have they not known: There is no fear of God before their eyes. Now we know that what things soever the law saith, it saith to them who are under the law: that every mouth may be stopped, and all the world may become guilty before God. Therefore by the deeds of the law there shall no flesh be justified in his sight: for by the law is the knowledge of sin. But now the righteousness of God without the law is manifested, being witnessed by the law and the prophets; Even the righteousness of God which is by faith of Jesus Christ unto all and upon all them that believe: for there is no difference: For all have sinned, and come short of the glory of God" (Rom. 3:9-23).

In verse 13 he draws attention to our poisonous lips. The asp was probably the Egyptian cobra. It is a very poisonous snake found in the desert and in the fields. ". . . The poison of vipers is on their lips" (Rom. 3:13;NIV). The natural thing for a man to do is to strike out and let the other person have the poison from his lips. In verse 19 he tells us that we have not known the way of peace. The way of peace does not flow naturally.

We read this passage and think . . . it means the wicked! It means them! Yes, it does! But it also means me. It means you. That is who Jeremiah meant when he said that the heart is wicked. It is naturally bent on doing evil. So there we have it. All the ingredients of killing a relationship are right there waiting to strike its victim.

Isaiah's experience with the Lord in the temple reveals the inner condition of humanity before a holy God. Isaiah was considered a man of integrity. He was one of those people who had his program together. It would appear that he had a good self-esteem about who he was. As long as he could compare himself to others, he could maintain a good opinion of his own character. As long as he compared himself with the standard of people, he could assure himself that he was no worse than his friends.

Something happened that totally reversed his view of himself. Something happened that caused him to come apart. *He had a glimpse of God!*

"In the year that king Uzziah died I saw also the Lord sitting upon a throne, high and lifted up, and his train filled the temple. Above it stood the seraphims: each one had six wings; with twain he covered his face, and with twain he covered his feet, and with twain he did fly. And one cried unto another, and said, Holy, holy, holy, is the Lord of hosts: the whole earth is full of his glory. And the posts of the door moved at the voice of him that cried, and the house was filled with smoke. Then said I, Woe is me! for I am undone; because I am a man of unclean lips, and I dwell in the midst of a people of unclean lips: for mine eyes have seen the King, the Lord of hosts" (Isa. 6:1-5).

A significant event happened to Isaiah. He "saw the Lord sitting upon a throne, high and lifted up, and his train filled the temple." Then he heard the song of the seraphims as they cried one to another, "Holy, holy, holy, is the Lord of hosts: the whole earth is full of his glory." The seraphims' emphasis is on the holiness of God. Their song makes God three times holy.

R.C. Sproul explains the reason for using the word holy three times. "On a handful of occasions the Bible repeats something to the third degree. To mention something three times in succession is to elevate it to the superlative degree, to attach to it emphasis of super importance.

"The Bible says that God is holy, holy, holy. Not that He is merely holy, or even holy, holy. He is holy, holy, holy. The Bible never says that God is love, love, love. It does say that He is holy,

holy, holy, the whole earth is full of His glory."[4]

Now when Isaiah saw the holiness, the purity, and the perfection of God, he cried out "Woe is me." When a prophet used the word woe, it was an announcement of doom. When he saw the Lord, he pronounced the judgment of God upon himself. Then he cried out, "For I am undone." The man who had it all together, suddenly unraveled and broke.

When he measured himself by God's standard, his goodness was completely shattered and destroyed.

As Isaiah realized his goodness was shattered and ruined, he cried out, "I am a man of unclean lips."

Isaiah cried out a basic truth and principle all believers need to realize. I am a person of unclean lips. I utter words that are poisonous and destructive. When I compare the utterance of my lips to a holy, holy, holy God, I am undone — I am unclean.

If you are a believer, you may say to yourself, "But I am a Christian. The Bible says, 'Therefore if any man be in Christ, he is a new creature: old things are passed away; behold, all things are become new' (2 Cor. 5:17). Since I am a new person in Christ, all things are new and I am changed from head to foot. I am with the folks that sing about the glory train. I am on the train headed for glory."

I am concerned with how believers become satisfied with accepting Christ, and believing that this one act of faith changes every aspect of their life. Simply being a born-again believer does not give you a deep meaningful relationship with others. Some of the meanest people I know claim to be Christians headed for heaven. There are those who claim to be new creatures in Christ that are as mean and bitter as those who are not heaven bound. Within the same congregation are some who are bitter with each other. They hold grudges, they are envious, they are jealous. They bite and devour each other. Their tongues spew poison at each other. They give each other the cold shoulder and a pouting face.

In a Japanese prison during World War II, there were a great number of missionaries in the camp. People reacted to the camp's pressures by treating others with cold indifference. James Holt wrote, "Many Christians were just as selfish as the others, fueling divisions and strife."[5]

Is the Scripture wrong when it says we become new creatures in Christ? No! Absolutely not!

Before you accepted Christ as your personal Saviour, your sins were not forgiven. You were on the train of sin that was headed for hell and destruction. You realized where you were heading, and called on the name of the Lord. You chose to accept Jesus Christ, get off the train headed for hell, and entered the door of forgiveness onto the glory train. When you took your seat on the glory train, you had a brand new position. Your spiritual position was now in Christ Jesus. You were no longer sitting in the old immoral and spiritually-damned seat where you had been seated before.

However, getting a new seat, a new position in Christ, does not mean that you have had a total heart operation on how to behave on the glory train. There is an interesting footnote on that verse in the King James Bible. It reads like this, "Therefore, if any man be in Christ, let him be a new creature" (2 Cor. 5:17).

Here is the point. Even though you have accepted Jesus Christ, you are on the glory train, and your sins are forgiven; that of itself does not mean you have done business with God, and dealt with the desperate wickedness that is in your heart. It does not mean that you have had your poisonous tongue depoisoned and tamed. It does mean that believers need a radical head operation in all areas of life.

Our heart, our very nature, is polluted with sin. We, by our very nature, respond wrongly in difficult circumstances. This is a fact we must grasp and clearly understand if we want to have better relationships with others. We must understand this in order to respond properly to God and experience the work of His Spirit in transforming our lives into the likeness of Jesus Christ.

This third principle in good relationships is that the wrong action and reactions come naturally, with no effort on our part. We naturally throw the sand instead of applying the oil.

Chapter 4

The Holy Limp

Even though you have accepted Jesus Christ, and your sins are forgiven; that of itself does not mean that all your actions have been depoisoned, and your tongue tamed. It does mean that believers must continue to bring all their actions, reactions, thoughts, and words under the authority and control of Jesus Christ. This often means a radical heart operation in all areas of our life.

My son Eldon had a dog named Lassie. Eldon and Lassie had a very good relationship. When he came home from school, Lassie ran to the van to meet him. There she was greeted with kind words and affectionate touches. Lassie followed her beloved master into the house, where she was treated to something out of the refrigerator. Lassie liked being with Eldon, and he liked being with her.

Something sad happened to this relationship. Lassie developed a heart problem. The choices were either to end the relationship, or give Lassie extensive and expensive treatment.

Lassie had heartworm. The problem starts when a mosquito draws blood from an infected dog. Circulating in the blood are tiny, immature worms called microfilaria. Once they are ingested by a mosquito, they undergo a series of changes, or molts.

Within two or three weeks, the microfilaria are transformed into infective larvae inside the mosquito. Then the next time the mosquito gets his blood dinner from another dog, that dog becomes infected. The deposited larvae travel to the dog's heart, where they mature into adult worms. There the adult worms grow as long as 14 inches. Once lodged in or near the heart, the female worm may deposit as many as 5,000 microfilaria into the dog's bloodstream, ready for the next mosquito to carry to another dog. Unless extensive treatment is given to first kill the heartworm and the microfilaria, the dog will most likely die. This kind of heart problem requires a major treatment to bring it under control.[1]

Born into humanity's bloodstream are all the larvae necessary to produce relationship destroying worms in our hearts. Unless we take extensive measures and follow with preventive treatment, we will continue infecting others and they will become relationship casualties in our lives.

Remember, the Bible likens our natural instinct to the poisonous cobra. As we follow our sinful nature, we instinctively spew out relationship-destroying poison. We do this because in our hearts are sinful worms producing larvae which hatch into destructive behavior. Implanted and lodged deep within the heart is the poisonous worm of selfishness. This is the worm within that wants its own way. As we tighten our grip to get what we want for ourselves, we lose our hold on good relationships.

The correction of this problem requires that we undergo a radical heart treatment. This brings us to the fourth principle in what it takes to "live peaceably with all men." We must learn that building good relationships takes hard work. While destructive behavior comes naturally, all the traits of building good relationships take persistence, conscience, and willful effort and sacrifice. Good relationships require regular and constant care. They are like anything else that is to function smoothly, they require constant maintenance. Good relationships require work. They will not flow naturally! Good relationships require sacrificing, and at times suffering on behalf of the other person.

This principle of sacrifice and hard work, starts with one of the hardest experiences required of believers. It really starts from an experience of repentance, and then flows out in a continual, ongoing walk of life. It becomes a daily part of the believer's walk in maintaining good relationships.

What is it? Is it accepting Jesus Christ and being born again? While this is a must to belong to the kingdom of Heaven, that of itself is not the fourth principle. Being heaven-bound on the glory train does not necessarily mean you have experienced this principle.

Is it a course in psychology, a visit to the psychiatrists couch, or reading positive thinking books? No! Some of these may have their place. However, they must follow the experience of the fourth principle to be effective in our daily lives, and to have godly relationships.

So what is it? It is killing the heartworm that keeps hatching and producing the poisonous cobra spirit deep within our inner being. It is the taming and depoisoning of our tongue. It is coming to the end of ourselves, and turning brokenheartedly to God for renewal. It means laying down self, and taking the way of Jesus Christ.

Jesus said, "If any man will come after me, let him deny himself, and take up his cross, and follow me. For whosoever will save his life shall lose it: and whosoever will lose his life for my sake shall find it" (Matt. 16:24-25).

The Bible says, "Likewise reckon ye also yourselves to be dead indeed unto sin, but alive unto God through Jesus Christ our Lord. Let not sin therefore reign in your mortal body, that ye should obey it in the lusts thereof. Neither yield ye your members as instruments of unrighteousness unto sin: but yield yourselves unto God, as those that are alive from the dead, and your members as instruments of righteousness unto God. Know ye not, that to whom ye yield yourselves servants to obey, his servants ye are to whom ye obey; whether of sin unto death, or of obedience unto righteousness?" (Rom. 6:11-13,16).

To deny yourself, to take up the cross of Jesus, and lose your life in Him requires a major heart operation. To reckon yourself to be dead to sin, and alive to Jesus Christ is more than a minor salve and band-aid application.

The Bible gives us a number of examples that will help us understand this principle and realize what God desires in the lives of believers.

The life of Jacob is one illustration.

Jacob was a schemer. He plotted and fought for his own way. Through a scheme, he stole the birthright from his older brother, Esau. Esau's cobra spirit of anger welled up within when he realized what happened. He set out to kill his brother Jacob. Jacob fled for his life!

He found acceptance with his uncle, Laban, and spent 20 years with him. There he schemed to deceive Laban. He was still a fighter at heart. His selfish attitude and independent spirit still stood in his way. His reliance upon himself kept him from resting his faith in God.

Now after all these years of scheming he must meet the brother from whom he fled. Jacob and Esau must meet face to face. Twenty years of scheming must now meet with 20 years of repressed anger. How is it going to come about? Jacob resorts to human psychology, and goes back to scheming.

"And Jacob went on his way, and the angels of God met him. And when Jacob saw them, he said, This is God's host: and he called the name of that place Mahanaim. And Jacob sent messengers before him to Esau his brother unto the land of Seir, the country of Edom. And he commanded them, saying, Thus shall ye speak unto my lord Esau; Thy servant Jacob saith thus, I have sojourned with Laban, and stayed there until now: And I have oxen, and asses, flocks, and menservants, and womenservants: and I have sent to tell my lord, that I may find grace in thy sight" (Gen. 32:1-5).

Jacob sent messengers, someone else, to meet Esau first. He instructed them to tell Esau about his achievements while he was with Laban. He told them to tell about his wealth and possessions, and about his servants. Perhaps Jacob thought to himself, *Maybe he will be impressed with my accomplishments, and because of all that I have, he will be forced to respect me. Or maybe he will realize that I am rich, and have no desire to fight for his wealth.*

It did not work. Esau was coming with 400 men. It looked like it was going to be a fighting reunion.

"And the messengers returned to Jacob, saying, We came to thy brother Esau, and also he cometh to meet thee, and four hundred men with him" (Gen. 32:6).

Jacob's spirit began to mellow and bend. He was "greatly

afraid and distressed." Out of fear of being killed, along with his family, he called upon God. He reminded God of the covenant that He had established earlier. This prayer was for deliverance from the anger of Esau. However, the prayer did not include the expression and utterance of a broken spirit. He called for help from God, then went back to scheming

He was not ready to send a message to Esau, saying, "Your brother Jacob realizes he has sinned against you and God. He is distressed, brokenhearted, and guilty. Esau, only your mercy and forgiveness will reunite you with him."

No, he did not do that! He went back to scheming, back to fighting! It may be somewhat nicer, and more "Christian" now. He plans, "I will send him 580 animals. I will appease him with the present that goeth before me, and afterward I will see his face, perhaps he will accept me."

It is getting better. What Jacob is doing is better than an outright fight. It is certainly a "positive" thing to do. But it is not quite what God wants yet. They are not ready for a godly reconciliation. God is not finished yet. Jacob and God have some very important business to do yet.

Jacob's problem is his self-will, self-purpose, his self-righteousness, self-desire, and self-defense. There is too much fight left in him to meet his long time enemy and brother. He was still fighting — but this time it was with God. God had been waiting on Jacob for 20 years. Now in a direct conflict, He is giving Jacob all night to surrender himself, to get the fight out.

Jacob had to learn the hard way. His opponent crippled him, and he was forced to give up. He was forced to realize his human weakness. God gave him a holy limp (see Gen. 32:24-32).

Now the fight is over. Jacob is reckoned as dead. The fight is gone. He is ready for the big task. He is now ready to go, with a holy limp to meet Esau; with no big army, no force, no bribe, no scheme. Nothing but a broken spirit, a surrendered heart, and a holy limp.

What happened when they met? An exhausted, contrite Jacob limped toward Esau, and bowed himself to the ground seven times. Esau's heart was touched. The fight left him, too. He ran and embraced Jacob, kissed him, and wept.

What a reunion! What reconciliation! Jacob helps us to understand the principle of self-denial, and that the things which build good relationships take diligent work and effort. Good relationships in the life of the believer require a "holy limp."

Something very interesting follows with Jacob's sons. We may hope they would have known of the lesson Jacob learned. But they did not. It was not a personal experience for them. They sold their brother Joseph, planned a cover-up, and lied to their father, Jacob. They, like their father, went on a 20-year guilt trip.

But God was not finished. A famine sent these brothers to Egypt to buy food. God wanted them reconciled to Joseph. He worked through their conscience and in their innermost being until they ran out of self-rope. They came to Joseph's house, and "fell before him on the ground." They did not only have a holy limp, they also had a holy fear. They begged for mercy. Then they were ready for Joseph to say, "I am Joseph, your brother."

They kissed, hugged, wept, and talked as they were reconciled. Their holy limp and holy fear brought them together again. Now please get this. This had to be an experience of their own. Hearing their father's story was not enough.

There is something else very important. Their holy limp and their holy fear was seen by God, and by the offended brother. Jacob's brokenness was seen by God, by his brother, and by the anxious spectators. There is no such thing as experiencing brokenness before God, and not expressing it to our fellow man. If you have not experienced the holy limp and holy fear before men, then you have not experienced it before God, either.

Let's go back to Isaiah. Isaiah saw the holiness and perfection of God. He cried out "Woe is me, I am ruined! I am a man of unclean lips!" He was undone, he came apart, he was shattered. He saw that he lived with a nation of dirty mouths, and that he was one of them. He was totally broken as he saw his sinful and helpless condition before God.

God extended grace, and would not allow His servant to remain without comfort. He cleansed Isaiah's lips, and restored his soul. One of the seraphim flew to the altar, and with tongs picked up a coal, too hot for even an angel to touch, and flew to Isaiah.

R.C. Sproul describes the experience like this. "The Seraph pressed the white-hot coal to the lips of the prophet and seared them. The lips are one of the most sensitive parts of human flesh, the meeting point of the kiss. Here Isaiah felt the holy flame burning his mouth. The acrid smell of burning flesh filled his nostrils, but the sensation was dulled by the excruciating pain of the heat. This was a severe mercy, a painful act of cleansing. Isaiah's wound was being cauterized, the dirt in his mouth was being washed away. He was refined by holy fire.

"He was cleaned throughout, forgiven to the core, but not without the awful pain of repentance. He went beyond cheap grace, and the easy utterance, 'I am sorry.' He was mourning for his sin, overcome with moral grief, and God sent an angel to heal him. A second of burning flesh on his lips brought a healing that would extend to eternity. In a moment, the disintegrated prophet was whole again. His mouth was purged. He was clean."[2]

Isaiah's lips were refined by holy fire. Holy lips are essential for good relationships.

Where are your holy lips when your son spills Coke on your new carpet? Or, when your teenage son sets his model on the stand your grandfather owned, and scratches it? Or, what happens when you do not get your way at the board meeting? Do you wound the spirit of others with your venom? Are relationships priority, or is some tangible thing, or getting your own way, or being on top, more important to you?

Look again at the teaching of Jesus I referred to earlier: ". . . If any man will come after me, let him deny himself, and take up his cross, and follow me" (Matt. 16:24).

While the experiences of Jacob, his sons, and the prophet Isaiah have shown us what this principle means, we dare not overlook the fact that Jesus Christ himself became the supreme example for us. The Bible teaches us that He gave everything on this earth in order to establish a living relationship between himself and humanity.

"Let nothing be done through strife or vainglory; but in lowliness of mind let each esteem other better than themselves. Look not every man on his own things, but every man also on the things of others. Let this mind be in you, which was also in Christ

Jesus: Who, being in the form of God, thought it not robbery to be equal with God: But made himself of no reputation, and took upon him the form of a servant, and was made in the likeness of men: And being found in fashion as a man, he humbled himself, and became obedient unto death, even the death of the cross. Wherefore God also hath highly exalted him, and given him a name which is above every name: That at the name of Jesus every knee should bow, of things in heaven, and things in earth, and things under the earth; And that every tongue should confess that Jesus Christ is Lord, to the glory of God the Father" (Phil. 2:3-11).

Jesus was the supreme example. He was not obsessed with preserving His reputation. He took the role of a servant, and stooped to wash the others' smelly feet. He humbled himself to become the sacrifice for our sins. He became obedient, even unto death. He carried the shame of others as He hung on the cross. He laid down everything for our good. He gave up all earthly possessions, and was hung on the cross in open shame, not even having a garment to cover His body.

What happened? Then God exalted Him! God gave Him a name with the highest reputation possible.

How important is this holy limp principle? My friend, it is very basic, it is a must for long, ongoing relationships.

The puzzle can become complicated. You have this nice couple that moves into your neighborhood. They are both very nice in short social contacts, or in public life. The shock comes when she leaves her "nice" husband, and begins living with another man who lives several blocks away. What is the problem?

The niceness is only a veneer pasted over the old nature. It is like a few good social rules glued over the old poisonous cobra nature that is deeply rooted inside. When the pressure of two self-natured people got too close, the veneer broke, and the old nature burst out. As the veneer split, deadly poison seeped out and destroyed the relationship. There was no holy limp, no holy fear, and no holy lips to hold them together.

Human thinkers can tell you how to paste on the veneer. I believe modern psychology has several missing links. The holy limp is a major missing link. After we experience our holy limp and holy lips, then we are ready for the nice social veneer.

Do you want to be a friend of Jesus Christ? Do you want to be a friend to those in the Church, and others around you? Then deny yourself, take up the cross, and meet your friends with a holy limp and holy lips.

Chapter 5

Love Covers, Hatred Cancels

On March 22, 1897, another baby girl was born to my grandparents. When she was three years old, she was placed in a foster home. At 16 years of age, she was afflicted with polio. This crippled her right arm and leg, and as a result she remained an invalid the rest of her life. She was forced to use crutches to move around in her home. Here was a young lady, crippled for life, wearing braces, and using crutches to get around. In spite of these handicaps, an amusing, young, red-haired country boy nick-named Red befriended her. It was not long until my Aunt Emma married Uncle Red. Why would any young person marry an invalid that he would need to carry from the house to the car every time they wanted to go away?

There was a father who had two sons. This man worked hard to make his way through life. His younger son became rebellious, and wanted to leave home. So he requested his share of the property, and his father granted it to him. The son went and blew it with his reckless and sinful living. His life was a disgrace to the reputation of his father. He had wronged his father, and used his inheritance very disrespectfully. And yet, when his father saw the son returning home, he ran to meet him, threw his arms around him, and kissed him. What was it that drove this father to overlook the sins of his son, and welcome him home again?

Seventeen-year-old Julie felt cut off from her parents. Her final, distressing words were just a glimpse of the despair that covered her like a shroud.

> Dear Diary,
> No one knows I'm alive, or seems to care if I die. I'm a terrible, worthless person and it would have been easier if I'd have never been born. Tabby was my only friend in the world and now she's dead. There is no reason for me to live any more.[1]

This was the note she left before she committed suicide. What was the driving force behind this tragedy, and so many other suicides today?

Another person expressed the feelings of a strained relationship like this, "It really hurts me to think the friendship we had is gone. If only I was given a reason. I feel rejected and hated. The feeling of being hated goes with me wherever I go. I can't get away from it. It even follows me to work."

What makes this nagging problem hang on?

> The phone rang in the home of high society Boston. On the other end of the line was a son who had just returned from Vietnam and was calling from California. His folks were the pseudo-cocktail circuit, wife-swapping party kind. The boy said to his mother, "I just called, Mother, to tell you that I wanted to bring a buddy home with me."
>
> His mother said, "Sure, bring him along for a few days."
>
> "But, Mother, there is something that you need to know about this boy. One leg is gone, one arm's gone, one eye's gone, and his face is quite disfigured. Is it all right if I bring him home?"

His mother said, "Bring him home for just a few days."

The son said, "You didn't understand me, Mother. I want to bring him home to live with us."

The mother began to make all kinds of excuses about embarrassment and what people would think . . . and the phone clicked.

A few hours later the police called from California to Boston. The mother picked up the phone again. The police sergeant at the other end said, "We just found a boy with one arm, one leg, one eye, and a mangled face, who has just killed himself with a shot in the head. The identification papers say he is your son."[2]

What drove this boy to hold that gun to his head? What was missing in Julie's life? Why does a person need to drive to work, feeling hatred?

Why would a young man marry a woman who was an invalid with braces and crutches?

Why would a father welcome home a son who had sinfully wasted his inheritance?

I believe the Scriptures will give us a clue to these questions.

"The end of all things is near. Therefore be clear minded and self-controlled so that you can pray. Above all, love each other deeply, because love covers over a multitude of sins. Offer hospitality to one another without grumbling" (1 Pet. 4:7-9;NIV).

Here is an important clue. *Love covers over a multitude of sins.* *Love* for the lady with crutches was like a blindfold for Red that covered or overlooked the physical handicaps of my Aunt Emma.

The father *loved* his prodigal son. Therefore, when he saw him coming a long way off, love compelled him to run and be reconciled to his son.

Julie and the Vietnam veteran were not feeling a strong love that covered their faults.

The individual experiencing rejection was feeling the withdrawal of love expressions from friends.

Whenever I have the assurance from another that I am deeply loved, I find it easy to keep no record of their wrongs and faults. When I feel rejected and hated, the other's faults become uncovered, and pop out like disturbed bees out of their hive.

When I express love to another, the faults and wrongs move for cover. Whenever I express resentment and envy, the other person begins to look like a full brother to the chief of sinners.

The Bible teaches that the believer is, above all else, to keep fervent love. The word fervent suggests putting forth effort like an athlete. It speaks of a strenuous and sustained effort. It is like a ballplayer putting all his effort into winning the game. The Bible commands believers to put forth strenuous effort into loving one another.

The reason is "Love covers a multitude of sins. Love does not keep a record of wrongs" (1 Cor. 13:5;TEV).

"Above all things have intense and unfailing love for one another, for love covers a multitude of sins — forgives and disregards the offenses of others" (1 Pet. 4:8;AMP).

When I feel loved, I can handle a multitude of offenses. Love expressed to me covers a multitude of sins in my outlook. It makes a big difference in how I perceive the other person. It triggers an attitude in my mind. When I feel loved, the sender of love signals looks more like a saint than a chief of sinners. When I feel loved, I feel like tackling the tough problems that go along with being a pastor and bishop. Feeling love works like putting dry kindling on a fire.

Solomon put the issue into perspective. "What a man desires is unfailing love . . ." (Prov. 19:22;NIV).

Flipping the coin now, when I express love to others, it too covers a multitude of sins in my own life. Love expressed to others helps overshadow and cover depression and discouragement. It overshadows those feelings of self-pity for myself because of all the responsibilities that rest on a bishop. It overshadows the temptation to throw in the towel. However you look at it, love expressed builds good relationships.

Jesus said, "A new commandment I give unto you, That ye love one another; as I have loved you, that ye also love one another. By this shall all men know that ye are my disciples, if ye have love one to another" (John 13:34-35).

There may be a tendency to interpret the call to love as a call to compromise biblical convictions, or to overlook sins that need to be corrected. This is not the case. Paul E. Billheimer made an important statement relating to that. "You are not compelled to surrender a personal conviction in order to love a brother, a member of the same family circle, who has the same Father." He continues, "We should understand that any issue that is controversial is potentially divisive unless hand-led with love."[3] What is love that covers?

It is not just a feeling. It is doing! It is something you do. It is giving words and deeds that communicate good. Alan Loy McGinnis gives an oversimplified illustration that has a valid point:

> I talked to a man whose marriage had gone bad after 18 years.
>
> "How did you know it was over?"
>
> "When she stopped putting toothpaste on my brush in the mornings," he replied. "When we were first married, whoever got up first would roll toothpaste on the other's brush and leave it lying on the sink. Somewhere along the line we stopped doing that for each other, and the marriage went downhill from there."

Another point he makes is very significant in my personal relationship book of rules. "One of the best ways to deepen a friendship is by eating together. It is no accident that so many important encounters occurred between Jesus and His friends when they were at the table. There is something almost sacramental about breaking bread with another. Have you ever noticed how difficult it is to have dinner with enemies and remain enemies?"[4]

There is something binding when we all put our feet under the same table, give thanks together, and share a tasty dish of food. When you and your friends stop eating together, it may be your friendship is in trouble. It may be a signal to give priority to resolving the difficulties.

Love expressed is helping another do some unpleasant task, and getting it done in half the time. Love is sending and receiving greetings at appropriate times that say, "I love you." Love is basically a lifestyle. It is the deeds you do, it is the words you say.

Our Lord spent a lot of time eating and visiting with common folk to teach us that love is proven more by etiquette than by eloquence.

What we love usually manages to get into our conversation. What is down in the well of the heart will come up in the bucket of speech.

Older people can live alone and stay healthy longer if they have close ties to family and friends.[5]

Hatred Cancels Out Love

Just a few words couched with a tone of resentment and bitterness sends a message to the hearer. The hearer receives the tone over the content of the words, and often feels hated and rejected. If there are no corrections made, if there are no signs of repentance, no apology, no loving deeds, no signals of love, the hearer then has an inner struggle on hand. Am I hated? Why? Now what's wrong? Several drops of animosity and hatred can cancel out a full clear glass of love. A drop of bitterness expressed will cloud over a whole life of love.

It took only one sin to destroy Adam and Eve's relationship with God. It took only one sin in Cain's heart to accumulate more sin and drive him to murder his brother.

When the ingredients of love that are expressed in daily living are missing or withdrawn, your relationship is in trouble. One sentence of hatred can erase a whole volume of love. Love and relationships are fragile. Handle with care and prayer!

The controversial auto maker, John DeLorean, had a keen understanding of this principle. "Another problem we faced was with the dealers themselves. Many felt they were being mistreated by Chevrolet and frequently they were. In turn, customer complaints about dealers were also high . . . . In most instances, the problem is quite minor, and the customer is not out of line in what he or she is asking. But when that customer is not treated with respect, then suddenly every minor rattle and slight flaw in workmanship becomes a major problem. Soon the owner is attacking the entire car line, turning away other potential customers, and creating serious problems."[6]

I find my attitude toward cars interesting. If there is a minor rattle under the dash, or a tailpipe hitting the frame with an annoying vibration, it makes the whole car seem like a clunker. Just one rattle under the dash can affect my feeling about the entire car. When I finally get that rattle fixed; however, it changes my attitude about the car. It seems like a good car again.

Love does cover a multitude of sins. However, when we withdraw love signals, or send messages that communicate hatred and rejection, the entire relationship begins to feel like a clunker to the hearer.

Don Baker points out how criticism can trigger his feelings. "I can get a hundred compliments only to have them all erased by one criticism. I can hear a hundred people say 'I love you,' and have them all buried beneath one intimidating frown."[7]

A person who feels hated or rejected feels like running away, throwing in the towel, or climbing the next jet and getting off on the other side of the world. For some it may be a suggestion of suicide, a wish just to die.

A lack of love stirs up all kinds of sins in your life, and the lives of those around you. A person who feels hated is like a swollen infected sore on the hand. Every little bump seems to hurt, and even expressions of love are interpreted through the sore spot. Whenever hatred enters a relationship, when friends feel the strain, rejection, or lack of love, a cloud begins to hover, and signals that a storm is brewing. Unless you have a firm grip on the four major principles I have shared with you, you will likely not know when your relationship develops rattles. If you know, you will probably not make corrections, either. You will be able to look back over your journey of life, and see relationship casualties behind you.

For some, it means divorce. For others, get another job, and still others, move to another church, or push your friends out of your social circle and search for new ones.

In order to express the fervent love that builds and binds together, keep these four principles in mind:

1. You must do something.
2. Make relationships a priority.
3. Be aware you naturally do what is wrong.
4. Good relationships take work and effort.

Exercise fervent, strenuous love one to another, for love covers a multitude of sins!

Chapter 6

Sin Separates

Sins of the heart drive people apart!

"Human beings are fragile and are easily broken."[1]

Adam and Eve were in the Garden of Eden enjoying the bliss of paradise. They were happy and loved each other. Their surroundings were perfect and beautiful. They were spotless and sinless before their Creator. Then something separated them from fellowship with God.

It was sin! Sin separates. Sin has been destroying relationships ever since. Sin is like sand in the bearings. It destroys marriages, family ties, friendships, partnerships, and neighbors.

The sins of the heart, the works of the flesh, are deadly poison in relationships. Sins of the heart destroy the character of the individual and cause others to recoil and look elsewhere for friendship. Sins of the heart separate people and kill relationships. Sins of the heart cause people to commit and express sin toward others. Expressed sins include acts of selfishness, unkind deeds, resentment, and sometimes even murder.

Cain became furious with his brother. Sin was crouching at his door. He murdered his brother Abel. Sin brought this brotherly relationship to an end, and left the parents in deep grief.

Jacob's sons hated their younger brother. ". . . they hated him and could not speak a kind word to him" (Gen. 37:4;NIV). "His brothers were jealous of him . . ." (Gen. 37:11;NIV).

Their hatred and jealousy led to 20 years of separation between Joseph and his brothers. It inflicted deep grief upon their father. It loaded these brothers with a guilty conscience, and sent their brother Joseph to jail. The sin of jealousy operating in their lives destroyed their character, and made life very difficult for others.

King Uzziah was prosperous and successful. God helped him win many battles, and his fame spread far and wide. He became a powerful king. Then the sin of pride and anger entered his heart. While he was expressing these sins by raging at the priests, leprosy broke out on his forehead. He then lived in a separate house, away from his friends until he died. The sins of pride and anger led to the separation of King Uzziah and his friends (see 2 Chron. 26).

Greed and lust for material things separated Gehazi from Elisha:

So Gehazi followed after Naaman. And when Naaman saw him running after him, he lighted down from his chariot to meet him, and said, Is all well? And he said, All is well. My master hath sent me, saying, Behold, even now there be come to me from mount Ephraim two young men of the sons of the prophets: give them, I pray thee, a talent of silver, and two changes of garments. And Naaman said, Be content, take two talents. And he urged him, and bound two talents of silver in two bags, with two changes of garments, and laid them upon two of his servants; and they bare them before him. And when he came to the tower, he took them from their hand, and bestowed them in the house: and he let the men go, and they departed. But when he went in, and stood before his master. And Elisha said unto him, Whence comest thou, Gehazi? And he said, Thy servant went no whither. And he said unto him, Went not mine heart with thee, when the man turned again from his chariot to meet thee? Is it a time to receive money, and to receive garments, and oliveyards, and vineyards, and sheep, and oxen, and menservants, and maidservants? The leprosy therefore of Naaman shall cleave unto thee, and unto thy seed for ever. And he went out from his presence a leper as white as snow (2 Kings 5:21-27).

Then Gehazi went from *Elisha's presence*. He got his perishable wealth, and neatly placed it in his house, but he lost his relationship with the man of God.

That is how sins of the heart work. They blind you to God's priorities and cloud your vision, hindering you from seeing that God's blessings are found in obedience and self-sacrifice.

David rescued Israel from the hands of the Philistines. He relieved Israel of the threat of the champion and giant, Goliath. He saved Israel from destruction and defeat, and safeguarded King Saul's role as king. King Saul in return gave David a high rank in the army. These two men should have been best of friends until the day of their death. David helped Saul more than any other person on the face of the earth. What a prospective team and close relationship!

Unfortunately, something happened!

David was being honored and praised for the great victory, and rightly so. As King Saul saw this transpiring, sin overtook him. He was overwhelmed with jealousy. Other sins like anger and dishonesty were evident in his life. He was so overtaken in sin that he sent men to David's house to keep watch, and kill him. David fled from Saul.

Sin had just destroyed another potentially beautiful relationship. Sin controlled Saul's life until he died.

Tragically, it did not stop there! King Saul's anger flared up at his son Jonathan. He called his own son the "son of a perverse and rebellious woman." He climaxed it by throwing his spear at him with the intent to kill. Sins of the heart destroyed his relationship with his own son.

Sin separates. Sin kills relationships.

Never entertain the thought that you can nurse hatred and jealousy toward one person, and contain it there. Hatred, envy, and jealousy toward any one person are sins of the heart. Heart sins spread poison wherever it makes contact. Sins of the heart cause your friends to leave you one after another. Sins of the heart are what leave relationship casualties lying along the road behind you.

It was sin in the heart of Judas Iscariot that drove him to the chief priests where he sold his friendship with Jesus for 30 pieces of silver. Sin cost him that relationship for all eternity.

Sins of the heart are serious! It splinters friendships for life, and sometimes for all eternity. Sin separates!

Jealousy is believed to have driven a man in Iowa to kill six relatives, and then himself. He was apparently enraged by the holiday attention showered on his sister and her three children. Sin made havoc of this relationship. Sin separates!

Richard Walters tells of a woman named Polly who was very jealous toward her own husband. She was "Jim's wife" in a very possessive way. She began to play detective, and made unfounded interpretations about Jim's behavior. She followed him, spied on him, and bugged him for details. Jim finally felt as if he were being driven out of the marriage. Suddenly, Polly was no longer Jim's wife.[2] Jealousy brought separation!

Sins of the heart drive people apart!

Sins of the heart drive people to the divorce courts!

Sins of the heart drive couples to live in the same house, but separated emotionally and spiritually.

Sins of the heart drive children to the nearest bus station to leave town.

Sins of the heart drive people to lawsuits.

Sins of the heart drive people to suicide.

Sins of the heart drive friends to throwing in the towel.

Sins of the heart drive churches into separate factions.

Sins of the heart drive people from job to job.

Sin is an evil slave master. It is like a boss who controls all you do, and the way you think. This slave master drives you to and fro on the face of the earth, never finding peace and happiness. Anger, jealousy, envy, pride, covetousness, selfishness, and competitiveness are all sins that destroy relationships.

Anger is the sin that would like to see misfortune fall on my enemy in revenge for wrongs.

Selfishness is the sin that must be in control of everyone and everything, or not play at all. Selfishness demands being right, and seldom accepts being wrong.

"Jealousy is the response we make when we fear that we will lose an object we desire. It is a painful cluster of feelings — fear, anger, shame, sorrow — and it often leads to thinking and behavior that is wrong."[3]

Tony Campolo says, "Envy is a desire to have what another person has. It is not simply a longing to have the same kind of thing the other person has; the envious person wants to strip another of something in order to possess it completely and solely."[4]

Envy is a real relationship breaker. We should fear it, and repent of it.

Pride is arrogant self-worship. It is the sin of exalting oneself and placing one's own interests above the interests of others. Pride craves admiration and even adoration, and will not share the limelight. Pride deludes its victims into believing that they have no peers and drives them to try to destroy anyone who takes recognition away from them. The proud are in love with themselves and seek to call attention to their admirable qualities.

"Pride keeps us not only from God, but from each other. Pride hinders us from being open and honest. *We would rather have people admire the selves we pretend to be than to love the selves we really are.*"[5]

Pride keeps you from confessing sins to your friends and relatives. Pride hinders you from saying, "I have wronged you, I am sorry."

King Saul's sins drove away his friends. Here is how it happened. First, he was selfish. His friendship was based on what others did for him. He had friends for his own personal benefit. Saul liked David because he could play his harp and cheer him.

Saul was possessive. David became very popular. Jonathan delighted in his friend David's popularity. But Saul was terrified by it, so he sought to possess David. "And Saul took him that day, and would let him go no more home to his father's house" (1 Sam. 18:2).

He cultivated jealousy. "And from that time on Saul kept a

jealous eye on David" (1 Sam. 18:9;NIV). He had jealousy in his heart, and he outwardly nurtured it by his behavior. What he *did* cultivated his heart sin, it acted like strong fertilizer.

Saul did not control his anger. He let it explode. Whether it is a slow crock-pot type anger cooking, or a gasoline explosion type, either will destroy relationships. One will slowly and surely, the other swiftly and certainly.

"A woman came to Billy Sunday and asked him to pray for her bad temper. Then, embarrassed by the admission, she justified herself by adding, 'But it's over in a minute.'

" 'So is a shotgun,' answered Sunday, 'But it blows everything to bits.' "[6]

Saul avoided the person who threatened and annoyed him. To end a relationship, do not talk about your hurts and problems. Simply avoid the person from whom they come as much as possible. Saul felt condemned by David's presence, so he avoided him. His presence reminded Saul of his spiritual need.

Saul cultivated envy. David was no longer a person to Saul. He was a competitor, and Saul envied him deeply.

Saul harbored hatred in his heart. His hatred was so deep that he tried to kill David. Saul was a miserable man, a man who was his own enemy. He died alone and in defeat.

Hatred divides, drives away, and separates people. Hatred causes everyone to lose.

Sins of the heart drive people apart. Sin is a hard slave master.

What can we do? Are we trapped forever? No, we can overcome!

1. Respond to the Holy Spirit's conviction! Recognize before God the sinfulness of your heart. Most of us readily admit we are "sorta sinners," but too few of us recognize the rotten sinfulness of our heart. God can help us when we recognize and confess our sinfulness to Him.

2. Confess and admit to others your struggles with heart sins. Many individuals do not find victory over sin's bondage by themselves. Do not spend the rest of your life in bondage rather than admitting and confessing your sins to others.

3. Seek forgiveness. Make corrections. Reconciliation with

others is a priority with God. It has a holy urgency to it.

4. Express love. C. S. Lewis wrote, "If you injure someone you dislike, you will find yourself disliking him more. If you do him a good turn, you will find yourself disliking him less."[7]

Jonathan and David were good friends. Their close relationship was built on meeting each other's needs. Anthony Campolo tells how this principle worked for him. "My wife is one of those rare people who always has compassion for wrongdoers, because she is concerned that their actions are expressions of their own unhappiness. Peggy persuaded me to be nice to my tormentor and to seek ways to make her feel good. I did my best. I took her to special denominational meetings, gave her public recognition for any positive thing she did for the church, and sent her postcards when I was on trips. I'm not sure how much all these kindnesses changed her feelings about me, but I do know that I was changed by them. Little by little, I realized that the more I did for that lady, the more I liked her. I learned what Jesus taught — the more I serve a person with whom I may justifiably be angry, the less angry I feel."[8]

Another time, a fellow named Dave took the proper steps to reconciliation. Nelson Coblentz told the story.

"I was handed a note with a first name, phone number, and 'Call by 9:15.' Heading for the phone I sensed an air of urgency but I didn't really know who I was to talk with nor the seriousness of the call. Placing the call I identified myself and in return came these words, 'Well, I am glad you called me, Nelson. You may not remember me, but about 17 years ago, I was going to kill you because I hated you, and I was serious! I'm Dave, a hairy, good-for-nothing bum, drunk; and tonight I was at your church meetings and . . . you talked about forgiveness and I couldn't handle it and halfway through I walked out. For 16 years I've not been to church except for a wedding or a funeral and . . . I haven't cried in years, but I am now, wow, I don't believe I'm doing this . . . but Nelson, can you forgive me . . . I am sorry."[9]

Reconciliation between Dave and Nelson took place. If only Saul would have done that! If only many more would do it!

If you need to make such a move — do it now!

Chapter 7

Shock Absorbers and Jesus

On our trip to Alaska we traveled the full stretch of the Alaska Highway. A portion of the highway was paved, but some other sections were muddy and rough. One particular stretch seemed to have no smooth track to drive on. It was filled with potholes. The sharpness of the bumps was hard on the shock absorbers. In fact, the rough drive ruined one of the front shocks. It almost sounded like it exploded.

There we were, way out in the wilderness country, far away from the local suburban auto parts store. What is the proper thing to do when a shock bursts? Replace it, of course. I can assure you, we found another shock and replaced it.

We had another option. We could have tried to make the rest of the journey with just three shocks. That would have been rough and dangerous. Still another option would have been to remove the other three shocks, and try to make the trip without anything to absorb the sharpness of the bumps. That would have been very foolish!

Imagine — one shock goes bad on your car, and to remedy it, you decide to pull the car into the garage, and remove the remaining shocks. Of course not!

Do you know what? That is what many people do with relationships. When the going gets rough and bumpy, and a shock absorber gets "knocked out," they remove all the shocks. Then they wonder why their relationships are strained and bumpy.

When relationship shock absorbers are needed most, we tend to pull them off. Something "bumpy" hits, something happens that does not please us, we did not get our own way, we did not win, or we could not be in control of the situation, so we just pull all the shocks and make life's journey much harder for our friends.

Pulling all the shocks is the wrong thing to do. To remove all the shocks is our first inclination and the natural thing to do. But it is wrong!

We treat our most precious gift in the world as a commodity to be bought, sold, picked up, or dumped off at our convenience. Some people would not think of treating their cars like they treat people.

Shock absorbers in relationships! What are they? What is that Christlike quality that smoothes out some of our rough spots, and helps us overlook being bumped and insulted? In China, it is a cup of tea! In America, it is a good cup of coffee, a cup of friendship. I can assure you a good cup of coffee or tea can soak up lots of angry feelings. Shock absorbers are lunch together, or an occasional picnic. It is dinner at our house, it is doing things together. It is interacting socially and helping one another. The Living Bible has this to say, ". . . let us outdo each other in being helpful and kind to each other and in doing good" (Heb. 10:24;LB).

Can't you just feel the superior quality of shock absorbers in such relationships? It is little wonder that the Scripture states, "Therefore, as we have opportunity, let us do good to all people, especially to those who belong to the family of believers" (Gal. 6:10;NIV).

Shock absorbers are doing nice things for those around you. Shock absorbers consist of compliments, words of encouragement, and expressions of approval and affirmation. Remembering someone's birthday or anniversary is an excellent way to show you care. Shock absorbers in relationships say, "I care about you. You are important to me. I realize that I bumped and bruised you, but I really care about you." Shock absorbers make, build, and bond relationships.

Often when we hit a bump in our relationships, we pull the plug on the coffee pot, discontinue dinner exchanges, drop the lunches, skip the kind deeds, forget the shopping trips, and cease to socialize — no more shock absorbers.

How often have you heard comments like these? "If that is the way they want to be, we'll just let them be that way, it goes home with them." "It's her problem. She'll have to give an account of her life." "If he wants to be that way, we just won't invite him anymore." "I was upset about the action, so I just figured they can go their own way." "I'm upset at him, I'll just let him go until he is good and ready to come back."

When something goes wrong in relationships, the first thing we see and feel is an objectionable quality in the other. Then we say if that is the way he or she wants to be, it is up to him or her. *I'll be spiritual* — I'll just take it and suffer. He can just go his own way — and so we push them off our hands. We let them hang on their lonely rope to twist in the wind until the relationship has shriveled. We just pull the shocks and let the relationship bounce to death.

Sounds rather noble, doesn't it? It is the natural thing to do. You have done it many times, haven't you?

So what is the problem?

1. It is not biblical. The Bible does not support it. It is the very opposite of scriptural teaching.

2. It is contrary to the teachings and examples of Jesus Christ.

3. It does not heal relationships. It deepens the hurts and pains. It widens the gulf of resentment and anger between people. It implants hostility and bitterness.

4. It does not foster growth, discipline, and maturity in each other. It does not build good Christian character.

Consider a relationship sermon conducted by Jesus Christ with His disciples:

> Take heed to yourselves: If thy brother trespass against thee, rebuke him; and if he repent, forgive him.

And if he trespass against thee seven times in a day, and seven times in a day turn again to thee, saying, I repent; thou shalt forgive him. And the apostles said unto the Lord, Increase our faith. And the Lord said, If ye had faith as a grain of mustard seed, ye might say unto this sycamine tree, Be thou plucked up by the root, and be thou planted in the sea; and it should obey you. But which of you, having a servant plowing or feeding cattle, will say unto him by and by, when he is come from the field, Go and sit down to meat? And will not rather say unto him, Make ready wherewith I may sup, and gird thyself, and serve me, till I have eaten and drunken; and afterward thou shalt eat and drink? Doth he thank that servant because he did the things that were commanded him? I trow not. So likewise ye, when ye shall have done all these things which are commanded you, say, We are unprofitable servants: we have done that which was our duty to do (Luke 17:3-10).

"Take heed to yourselves." "Be on your guard." When you see that statement, take special notice! It is like those bumpy corduroy-like noise makers near a dangerous intersection on the road. They are there to keep you awake, to get your attention. Jesus said, "Take heed." This indicates it is going to be hard and difficult. It will not be easy, but is very necessary. Jesus said, "If thy brother trespass against thee, rebuke him." The Amplified version reads, "If your brother sins (misses the mark), solemnly tell him so and reprove him."

That is very difficult to do, especially when you do it within the context of humility and divine love. However, notice that Jesus lays the obligation squarely on you — the victim. We would rather retort and say, "He wronged me, he is obligated."

This goes against our "grain," our nature. We react and say, "He wronged me, he is obligated. He needs to come to me, not me to him." We find it easier to go tell someone else.

Richard Strauss wrote, "If somebody has injured us, putting them in a bad light seems to us to be a fair way of retaliating, balancing the scales, and restoring some of our self-esteem. It can also be an effective way of winning people on our side in the conflict."[1]

Jesus is telling us that pulling the shocks, turning a cold shoulder, or putting a distance between us is *not* acceptable for Christians. These reactions are wrong, and violate the teachings of Jesus Christ.

Jesus said, "If thy brother trespass against thee, rebuke him." Rebuke means to reprove. It means to bring to light, expose, set forth; to convict or convince. It means helping the offender see the fault, in such a way that corrections can be made. It means confronting and helping your friend make amends.

Jesus said, "Moreover if thy brother shall trespass against thee, go and tell him his fault between thee and him alone: if he shall hear thee, thou hast gained thy brother" (Matt. 18:15).

In recent years, I have tried to give extra attention to people who have been emotionally hurt. I have met people who have been inflicted with an ongoing hurt because of breakdowns in relationships. It happens between close friends, family members, or people in the church. They experience a "pulling of the shocks," and the cold shoulder cut-off. I can just see the old grandmother, the sister, the brother-in-law, or the father, with tears flooding their eyes and running down their cheeks, crying "Why? If only I knew what I did, I would like to change. I would do anything to restore our *closeness,* but I do not know what to do. I don't know what I did." People are hurting because someone "pulled the shocks" in relationships, and they do not know why.

Jesus Christ taught that this kind of behavior is off limits. Pulling the shocks may be the easiest response for the moment. Taking heed and helping your friend make corrections is harder. But it is the right thing to do.

You say, "I don't want to be nit-picking on little things!" That is good. That is correct. Jesus Christ is not telling us that we should demand that people simply follow our wishes and do things the way we want. He is, however, giving us two options.

1. Bearing with each other in our annoying faults, rather than withdrawing fellowship. If it is not a sin against God, or people, then "bear with one another." Withdrawing fellowship

and pulling the shocks is not an option.

2. If the fault is destroying your fellowship or causing you to "cold shoulder it," Jesus obligates you to confront, rebuke, restore, and forgive.

In other words, it is either overlook it or resolve it. The wrong way is to suppress it and withdraw fellowship, and leave the other person bumped out of your way to suffer alone.

Jay Adams gives this fictional episode to illustrate this point:

> Mary has not seen Jane for some time since Jane has been out of town on vacation. Now Jane has returned. Mary spots her in church and determines to say hello after the service. After the benediction, Mary hurries to the other side of the church to where Mary had been sitting. By now Jane is on her way out of the church.

> Mary calls her, "Hello, Jane. Wait for me!"

> But Jane sticks her nose up in the air and sails out of the church as quickly as she can, without so much as "Howdy do" to Mary.

> Mary can respond in one of two ways. If she does what many Christians do, she will say "Hmmp! Well! If that's the way she wants to act, then let her go! She can come to me the next time. That will be the last time I go after her!" And so a friendship is ruined, the work of Christ is hindered as the Body is weakened, and the honor of God is compromised.

> But if Mary . . . is willing to obey Christ, she will not settle for that. Instead, she will follow Jane from the church and search her out.

> She says, "Jane! What's wrong? I was so glad to see you that I hurried over to your aisle and called you, but you stuck your nose in the air and left the church ignoring me, as if I didn't exist. What's wrong? I must tell you that I was greatly hurt."

> Jane responds, "Oh, Mary, I am so sorry! Let me explain. I was sitting through church thinking about

only one thing. I have a bad cold, and my nose began to run. But I had left my handkerchief here in the car. I was afraid that since the preacher preached so long I'd drip all over my new dress and my Bible . . . . so as soon as the benediction was over, I put my head back so I wouldn't drip and rushed to the car."

After a good laugh and a hug or two, Mary and Jane are reconciled.[2]

There was really no offense. It was only a misunderstanding. What a silly scenario, you say! Yes, it is — in a way. Yet Adams wrote, "I have counseled persons who were separated from each other for more than 20 years by some misunderstanding that was every bit as silly."

Offenses do come. We must accept that! The offended person knows there is a problem, even if the offender does not know, or does not know what the problem is. The offended is required to go. Jesus wants no loose ends. As Adams wrote, "He wants every personal difficulty between brothers resolved."

A true story is told of a mother-in-law and a daughter-in-law who had trouble accepting each other. The daughter-in-law was diagnosed with inoperable cancer and still struggled with the fragmented relationship as she became worse. Lying in bed one day, she asked her husband if he had heard the noise. He hadn't, so she described it to him. It was like a wall that came crumbling down. It was a symbolic expression of what had happened within her. The wall between her and her mother-in-law had fallen. Not long afterward, she died peacefully.[3]

There is a good side and a bad side to this story. The good side is that the wall was destroyed before she died. There was time for deathbed reconciliation. The bad side — Jesus wanted these two people to enjoy each other in life. They missed a real opportunity of having a meaningful relationship. Jesus wants us to live so we can enjoy each other's friendship and fellowship.

Often the most difficult causes of grief experienced through the death of a loved one are the "if only's" that were unresolved.

I do not believe that is the will of Jesus! He wants us to enjoy each other in life, then we will be ready for death.

Chapter 8

Solemnly Reprove — But How?

Bad relationships are devastating!

Relationships gone sour completely change one's way of life. That bad relationship becomes the dominant, evil, slave-driver of your life that controls you like a dictator. It controls your thoughts and actions, your plans, work, sleep, the places you go, and how and when you go. It even controls whether or not you go. You shuffle your life around your enemy like a plague to be avoided. In-law conflicts, envy toward a friend, or jealousy with a co-worker are slaves that control and dominate. Bad relationships control and dominate your actions.

That kind of behavior then becomes offensive and difficult for others. It hurts your friends, and keeps them at a distance.

Relationships gone bad limit the gifts of the Spirit that God has given to His children. The person who has it "in for dad" is destroying the quality of both their lives, and limiting their potential contribution to the Church. The people who constantly work against leadership, continually release their unfounded gripes about the pastor, and insist on doing it their way are really destroying their own ministry to the lives of others. Through bad relationships, Satan succeeds in limiting believers to build each other up in the faith through the gifts of the Spirit. When you are jealous of another, you do not exercise your gift to encourage and build up that person in the body of Christ. You do not affirm and encourage the other to excel in the gifts given to him or her by God.

Bad relationships control your life, and limit the working of the Holy Spirit in your life.

This is not the will of Christ for His church. He wants these faults corrected. Some seem to think it is more spiritual to suffer it out and look the other way, or just put it in the back of our minds. I can assure you Satan will see to it that it does not stay there.

Richard Strauss, in *Getting Along with Each Other*, explains why overlooking is not the answer.

> Some of us think it is more spiritual to ignore it and quietly put up with it.
>
> That may be true if we really could ignore it, if we could forget that it ever happened. But usually we don't. We let it eat at us. And our bodies keep score of the hurts we have suffered, and they make us physically ill. Or we let the resentment build and leak out in unexpected ways, corroding our relationships. Or it explodes in anger and unkind words that drive people away from us. Overlooking is not the answer.
>
> Furthermore, to allow ourselves to go on being manipulated or victimized by the faults of other people is to condone their selfish and sinful behavior, which will probably be directed at somebody else very soon (if it has not been already). So for the sake of the offender and our relationship with him, as well as for the protection of others who might be hurt, we need to stop making excuses for him and striving along with him, hoping things will soon get better. We need to be honest about his faults, and confront him.[1]

The question is how?

Jesus taught that if the fault is destroying the relationship, we are to attempt correction. It means helping the offender see his fault in such a way that correction can be made.

The question remains: How do we go about it? Strauss says, "But wait just a minute before you open your mouth. There is a condition you must meet first."

Let's look at several Scriptures that will help us learn God's way of confronting one who is at fault.

"And the Lord sent Nathan unto David. And he came unto him, and said unto him, There were two men in one city; the one rich, and the other poor. The rich man had exceeding many flocks and herds: But the poor man had nothing, save one little ewe lamb, which he had bought and nourished up: and it grew up together with him, and with his children; it did eat of his own meat, and drank of his own cup, and lay in his bosom, and was unto him as a daughter. And there came a traveller unto the rich man, and he spared to take of his own flock and of his own herd, to dress for the wayfaring man that was come unto him; but took the poor man's lamb, and dressed it for the man that was come to him. And David's anger was greatly kindled against the man; and he said to Nathan, As the Lord liveth, the man that hath done this thing shall surely die: And he shall restore the lamb fourfold, because he did this thing, and because he had no pity.

"And Nathan said to David, Thou art the man. Thus saith the Lord God of Israel, I anointed thee king over Israel, and I delivered thee out of the hand of Saul; And I gave thee thy master's house, and thy master's wives into thy bosom, and gave thee the house of Israel and of Judah; and if that had been too little, I would moreover have given unto thee such and such things. Wherefore hast thou despised the commandment of the Lord, to do evil in his sight? thou hast killed Uriah the Hittite with the sword, and hast taken his wife to be thy wife, and hast slain him with the sword of the children of Ammon. Now therefore the sword shall never depart from thine house; because thou hast despised me, and hast taken the wife of Uriah the Hittite to be thy wife. Thus saith the Lord, Behold, I will raise up evil against thee out of thine own house, and I will take thy wives before thine eyes, and give them unto thy neighbour, and he shall lie with thy wives in the sight of this sun. For thou didst it secretly: but I will do this thing before all Israel, and before the sun. And David said unto

Nathan, I have sinned against the Lord. And Nathan said unto David, The Lord also hath put away thy sin; thou shalt not die. Howbeit, because by this deed thou hast given great occasion to the enemies of the Lord to blaspheme, the child also that is born unto thee shall surely die" (2 Sam. 12:1-14).

"Brethren, if a man be overtaken in a fault, ye which are spiritual, restore such an one in the spirit of meekness; considering thyself, lest thou also be tempted. Bear ye one another's burdens, and so fulfil the law of Christ. For if a man think himself to be something, when he is nothing, he deceiveth himself. But let every man prove his own work, and then shall he have rejoicing in himself alone, and not in another. For every man shall bear his own burden" (Gal. 6:1-5).

With this scriptural background, let us put together some principles and applications on how to "solemnly . . . reprove," as Jesus taught in Luke 17:3.

1. Shock absorbers must be in place.

Galatians 6:1 gives instructions on restoring one taken in a fault. Following some direction on procedures we are warned, "But watch yourself, you may also be tempted" (NIV).

Strauss gives this valid point. "There is no way we can properly confront others with an air of superiority. Biblical confrontation is just one sinner sharing with another something that might make them both better people and make their relationship with each other stronger and more satisfying. Suggestions are easier to take from someone who lets you know he has the same weakness you have.

"But for the grace of God, we would be doing the same thing he is doing. In fact, we probably have. And we very well may again. Remembering *that* will keep us from a vindictive, condemning, holier-than-thou attitude, and will help us maintain a gentle, kind, and calm tone. Then the nets will be mended, and together we will fulfill God's purposes for our lives — ministering to each other's needs, contributing to each other's lives and building each other up for the glory of the Lord."[2]

God's people are commanded to encourage each other. We are to affirm one another's gifts and positions. If you are already an encourager to your friend, you are then in a position to solemnly help him make corrections.

However, if you have already done what comes naturally, and pulled the shock absorbers from your relationship, remember that restoration of friendships may well need to take place before Godly reconciliation can truly be experienced.

God sent the prophet Nathan to correct David. It was not just mere chance that Nathan was chosen. Nathan was able to confront David because he was the man who had earlier encouraged David to build the house of God. "And Nathan said to the king, Go, do all that is in thine heart; for the Lord is with thee" (2 Sam. 7:3). Nathan stood without fault before David. He had not cut the relationship off earlier, and then tried to make a correction.

A child needs the parents' love when it is least deserved. When a father disciplines his child, the child needs the assurance of acceptance and love. A wise parent will not discipline his child and send him to his room until he is done crying. The child needs to be held, loved, and accepted for the discipline to be most effective.

Adults are much the same. Helping others make corrections is nearly impossible if you have cut them off and rejected them. Too often "natural" things happen first, then we play the cut off, rejection, and avoidance game. Then we turn "spiritual" and want to patch up.

If, in your strained relationships, you have already pulled the shocks, and sent rejection signals, then you need to respond with repentance and confession. Repent of your rejecting attitude. Confess your sins to God, and receive His forgiveness. Move on and confess your rejection to the persons you cut off, and ask for forgiveness.

Chances are very high that if you do this, you will not need any additional steps in solemnly rebuking the other.

Too often, we fail to realize the high cost of discipleship at this point. We just continue passing our destructive faults on to our children and our grandchildren.

2. Get the facts.

"Brethren, if a man be overtaken in a fault . . . restore . . ." (Gal. 6:1).

"Paul is probably dealing with something into which a

person has fallen that will bring reproach on the name of Christ and the testimony of the Church. Other believers in the assembly are not simply to ignore it and hope it will disappear. They are to recognize it for what it is — a fault. The word means a false step, a blunder, a mistake or an error. It was probably not premeditated, but it was something that simply caught him off guard."[3]

Our friends are not normally out to slight us, or do us in, or hurt us. But sometimes they do, and may not be fully aware of what is happening. Or others in the body of Christ may be bringing reproach to His great name, or dissension within the Church, or influencing the Church in the wrong direction. An approach is necessary, but go with the facts!

I have often misinterpreted the true motives in other people's actions. My initial impression is often wrong. Again and again a suspicion has been cleared away with communication of a few simple facts. I have been misinterpreted many times, and my motives misjudged. As I see my own wrong interpretation of actions and how others at times misjudge me, I am reminded of the importance to get the facts as straight as possible. Trying to solemnly rebuke without the facts often ends up like a dead end street, getting you nowhere. It is risky and wrong to react on the first tip from the gossiper's mouth. It is dangerous to make an assumption on a small part of the picture.

As Nathan went to David, he went with the facts. He knew what David's sin was. He knew what had happened, and where David was wrong. He was able to confront and deal with David with facts David could not deny.

We notice that the Lord sent Nathan to confront David. I believe Nathan was perceptive and open to the facts because of his close walk with God. The closer we walk with God through understanding the Scriptures, the better will be our perception of the facts.

God wants the believer to walk closely with Him, so that he will become a partner with the Holy Spirit in discerning facts and correcting faults. The believer is to become the tool the Spirit uses in correcting faults in the Church. The cost of such a walk is often higher than many believers are willing to pay.

3. Use wisdom in timing.

Sometimes it is wise to make corrections on the spot. That is how the Holy Spirit directed the Apostles to handle the lying and deception of Ananias and Sapphira.

At times it may be wiser to use the method God used with Adam and Eve. He called for them in the cool of the day.

Always it is wise to first pray diligently, and lay the matter before the Lord, like Hezekiah did.

It is never wise to use the bantam rooster approach in timing, that is, striking at first impulse, with feathers ruffled, and quarrelsome, aggressive attitudes. Several meanings given in dictionaries for bantam are "a small quarrelsome person," and "a small, but aggressive person."

There is an interesting observation that we can learn from Nathan's approach to David. "We need to recognize that the Lord waited an entire year from that act of sin before He sent Nathan to David. That delay was not caused by cowardice, but by the recognition that sometimes we need to wait until the Holy Spirit has prepared that person's heart to hear God's Word. It is for that reason that we need to be dependent on the Lord's guidance, both as to whether we should go and when we should go. More than once I have thanked God that His Spirit held me back until it was His time, not mine."[4]

There is something important in this waiting period with David. The verdict is clear. Nathan told David, "The child also that is born unto thee . . . ." The child was already born to support Nathan's charge. Then comes the real heart breaker, "the child . . . shall surely die."

In God's own precise timing, the prophet brought two convicting and crushing announcements upon David. "Thou art the man" and "the child . . . shall surely die."

"David therefore besought God for the child; and David fasted, and went in, and lay all night upon the earth" (2 Sam. 12:16). The result of conviction and depth of repentance can be felt as you read Psalm 51. It is understandable why David cried out, "Have mercy upon me, O God . . ." (Ps. 51:1).

Notice also that Nathan was not hot with anger when he approached David. One reason for waiting is to be sure our anger has cooled off, and has been dealt with. The Bible teaches, "For the wrath of man worketh not the righteousness of God" (James 1:20). "For man's anger does not promote the righteousness God (wishes and requires)" (AMP).

I cannot recall any experience where a person's anger expressed has brought about a broken and contrite spirit. We must have utmost wisdom in our timing. In some situations, there never seems to be a right time. This requires making a decision to do the right thing, even though the atmosphere cannot be such as we would desire. Confronting must be carried out, even when it will be unpleasant.

4. Prepare your heart and words.

Jimmy and Johnny are playing together in the sandbox. They are good friends who play together five days out of seven. When Jimmy grabs the little dump truck Johnny is playing with, Johnny bursts out, "I hate you, I am going home!"

Jimmy replies, "I hate you, too! Go home!"

Billy and Bobby are playing in the back yard. They are having a great time pretending to be in the major leagues. Billy suddenly drops the ball, his smile turned upside down as he runs toward home. Bobby calls, "What's wrong, Billy?" Billy does not reply as he patters on home.

For every child's story like this, there are probably dozens of adult experiences to match them. We adults (even parents, leaders, or grandparents) behave much the same way. We send hate signals and leave the impression we are finished with the relationship. We send rejection signals when we really desire a closer friendship. Adults pout and make life miserable for others without telling them what is wrong. We throw our friends out and close the door, when what we really want is a pesky little fault corrected.

Let's take a closer look at these children's problems. The real problem in the sand box is that Johnny does not want the toy truck grabbed out of his hand when he is playing with it. That is reasonable and understandable. "I hate you" and the reply, "I hate you, too" are both big lies. Johnny did not hate Jimmy. He simply did not like to have the toy truck grabbed from him. He should have told him the truth with love. The truth is, "Jimmy, I don't like to have the truck grabbed out of my hand. It is not a nice thing for friends to do to each other."

Neither is Billy really mad at Bobby. But when he leaves so suddenly, Bobby is alone, trying to guess what could possibly be wrong, leaving him to explore dozens of options, and probably choosing the wrong one.

These children did what came naturally. They sent hatred and rejection signals when things did not go their way. Many adults never change the inherited pattern.

The Bible instructs believers to be truthful to each other.

"But speaking the truth in love, may grow up into him in all things, which is the head, even Christ" (Eph. 4:15).

"Wherefore putting away lying, speak every man truth with his neighbour: for we are members one of another. Be ye angry, and sin not: let not the sun go down upon your wrath: Neither give place to the devil. Let him that stole steal no more: but rather let him labour, working with his hands the thing which is good, that he may have to give to him that needeth. Let no corrupt communication proceed out of your mouth, but that which is good to the use of edifying, that it may minister grace unto the hearers. And grieve not the Holy Spirit of God, whereby ye are sealed unto the day of redemption. Let all bitterness, and wrath, and anger, and clamour, and evil speaking, be put away from you, with all malice: And be ye kind one to another, tenderhearted, forgiving one another, even as God for Christ's sake hath forgiven you" (Eph. 4:25-32).

William Backus wrote the book *Telling Each Other the Truth.* He makes this point in relation to Ephesians 4.

"In this chapter Paul describes the body of Christ. He says Christians, members of that Body, are connected to one another by joints. If these joints are arthritic so that contacts between members are abrasive and poorly lubricated, the Body itself will crack and falter. When the joints are working smoothly, the Body's movements will be effective and efficient. Truth is the *oil* which lubricates the joints in the body of Christ."[5]

The Smiths and the Joneses were long-time friends. They supported each other during tough times, and rejoiced with each other during joyous times. However, when socializing at the Smith's house, Mr. Jones would put his feet on Mrs. Smith's coffee table, and she did not like it. She boiled inside, and went to bed angry. There were no more invitations to the Smiths. The Joneses noticed, but did not know what was wrong. Bitterness grew and hurts increased. The conversations were reduced to mundane pleasantries as the problem multiplied into major emotional turmoil. If only Mrs. Smith would have told Mr. Jones that the coffee table had belonged to her grandfather, and that her grandmother had refinished it. She treasured her inherited gift, and found it difficult not to show her anger when he put his feet on it. That would have been a more appropriate way to deal with the frustration.

The Bible calls those who are spiritual to deal with the faults of others. One of the characteristics of a spiritual person is truthfulness. In order to make corrections in each other's lives, we are called to express truthfulness rather than pushing each other out the door and out of our lives.

Nathan was careful in his speaking to David. "He did not rush into David's presence and blurt out a condemnation, and neither did he approach David in a way that would humiliate him before others. It is obvious that Nathan had thought carefully both about what he would say and how he would say it. Nothing was more likely to pierce through David's defenses than a story about a poor shepherd and his pet lamb."[6]

We may not be as skilled as Nathan in making the point. However, if relationships are priority to us, we will be giving much attention to having a pure heart and speaking the truth in love. We may even decide that being friends is more important than owning grandfather's coffee table.

The problem is, speaking the truth in love, with kindness that says, "I care about you," *does not come naturally.* It requires repentance and submission to God's Spirit.

5. Restoration must be the definite goal.

Ricky Muncy lay in a coma for five weeks in the Fairfax Hospital. On August 4, 1987, his mother was taking Ricky home from a child care center, when a bag of cement fell from a truck she was following. As she swerved to miss it, she was forced onto the shoulder of the highway, and the car crashed into a tree. Ricky was found unconscious and without a pulse. He was flown to the

Fairfax Hospital and spent five weeks there in a coma. He was moved to a children's hospital in Washington, DC, where he received therapy and long-term care.

One year after the accident, Ricky was brought home to live with his parents. His homecoming was a celebration. He was greeted with welcome signs on the trees and the house.

What was the purpose in flying Ricky to the Fairfax Hospital? What was the goal of the doctors and nurses? What was the aim of the therapists? Restoration!

The aim of any rebuke must be correction and restoration. Galatians 6:1 says, "...restore such an one." "Restore him gently" (NIV). "You . . . should set him right and restore and reinstate him" (AMP).

The word restore means to put in proper condition.

When I was 12 years old, my younger brother and I were both riding the same horse when the strap on the saddle broke. We both fell off, and as a result, my arm was badly broken. I was rushed to the doctor, who reset the bone. It was put in a cast, where restoration and healing took place.

Galatians 6:1 speaks of a broken relationship that needs to be repaired.

God's purpose for His children is to bring people to Christ, and minister to the needs of those around them. When a believer's life is torn by faults, ministering to others becomes very limited. There needs to be mending and restoring. In many cases, restoration will not take place unless a Nathan confronts the faulty believer.

The Bible commands believers to admonish one another. "And I myself also am persuaded of you, my brethren, that ye also are full of goodness, filled with all knowledge, able also to admonish one another" (Rom. 15:14). "Let the word of Christ dwell in you richly in all wisdom; teaching and admonishing one another in psalms and hymns and spiritual songs, singing with grace in your hearts to the Lord" (Col. 3:16).

Admonish means to put in mind. It has the idea of facing someone with a fault, and warning him of the consequences of continuing in the wrong way. The purpose is to restore and bring healing to that ailing relationship.

The purpose of admonition is not to prove your point, to get even, to blame, or to make the other individual look bad. It is for the purpose of restoration!

We must remember that we are not the Holy Spirit. We are called, however, to submit to the desire of the Holy Spirit, and then carry out His goals and wishes. Nathan's approach to David carries with it the authority of the Holy Spirit and His method of approach. Nathan's aim was for restoration.

Nathan challenged David from the standard of God's Word. He pointed out David's ugly sin, and reminded him that it was a sin against God. "Wherefore hast thou despised the commandment of the Lord..." (2 Sam. 12:9). "And David said unto Nathan, I have sinned against the Lord..." (2 Sam. 12:13). The restoration Nathan sought began unfolding.

Jesus said, "... If your brother sins, rebuke him ..." (Luke 17:3;NIV). Rebuke means to bring to light, to expose, to set forth, or to convict or convince. This means to tell an offender his fault in such a way that he will be convinced, and will want to make correction. This is restoration. Aim for it.

6. Go in the attitude of gentleness and forgiveness.

The Bible says, "... restore such an one in the spirit of meekness..." (Gal. 6:1). "...Restore him gently..." (NIV). "You who are spiritual — who are responsive to and controlled by the Spirit — should set him right and restore and reinstate him without any sense of superiority and with all gentleness" (AMP).

There is little difference in the meaning of meekness and gentleness in the way the Bible instructs believers to practice them in their daily lives. Simply put, meekness is submission to the will of God. Therefore, go to *restore* your brother, with you yourself being fully submitted to the will of God. Gentleness means giving consideration to others even when they have wronged us. Gentleness means restraining the human nature that calls us to strike back, to tell him off, and give what he gave. "It keeps us from attacking even when we have the weapons to win. It is strength in control, like a mighty stallion held in check with bit and bridle. It is the attitude that restores."[7]

Gentleness will avoid the "I am right, you are wrong" fight. Any attempt to show yourself as right over against the other as wrong will not bring about desired restoration. Whenever the "I am right attitude" raises its head, it strikes up a defense mechanism in the other. The result is a fight rather than restoration.

It is like two bantam roosters meeting each other in the barnyard. One raises his feathers to signal that he is in control. The other returns the greeting, and the result is a fight. Any expressions of "I am right, therefore you are wrong" are deadly poison to any relationship. It is just like sand in a bearing. Such attitudes do not apply the oil of meekness from the Holy Spirit.

If you are just a little glad to see the other person proven wrong, your attitude is *sinful,* and will block any attempts at meaningful restoration. Jesus' heart was saddened when He saw people deliberately continuing in sin and evil. Sadness and grief should be our attitude toward those who will not acknowledge their wrongs and faults before God.

If you are out to prove people wrong, do not even expect to have meaningful friendships with others. Do not count on many long-time friends or close relationships. There is an ocean of difference between rebuking solemnly and biblically, or proving the other person to be wrong. The "I am right" attitude succeeds only in driving people from God, the Church, and you.

If you insist on manipulating and controlling, do not expect restoration. If you approach the problem from your opinion, do not expect restitution.

When Nathan came to David, he did not come with personal opinions or prejudices. He did not come to David to stomp on him. Rather, he came with a message that said, "Thus saith the Lord God of Israel." He was also prepared to tell David, ". . . The Lord also hath put away thy sin; thou shalt not die" (2 Sam. 12:13).

Restoration must be the aim!

7. Affirm with love.

Nathan demonstrated an affirmation of love and acceptance toward David. He did not go to David to "tell him like it was," and then reject him. He continued to cultivate his friendship with David.

Approximately a year after this confrontation, David and Bathsheba had another son. They named him Solomon, which means peaceful or peace. It was a name that declared David's acceptance of God's forgiveness. You will discover in 2 Samuel 12:25 that Nathan also gave a meaningful name, "Jedidiah, because of the Lord." That is, he is loved of the Lord.

Notice the close ties Nathan cultivated with David. He went so far as to give David's son a special name. Can you imagine the kinship David felt toward Nathan for giving such attention to his son? Unfortunately, too many believers today would have nothing to do with "David's son."

James Hilt draws attention to the approach Jesus used in comforting the seven churches. There are lessons for us to learn. Addressing the church in Ephesus, Christ said; "I know thy works, and thy labour, and thy patience, and how thou canst not bear them which are evil: and thou hast tried them which say they are apostles, and are not, and hast found them liars: And hast borne, and hast patience, and for my name's sake hast laboured, and hast not fainted. Nevertheless I have somewhat against thee, because thou hast left thy first love. Remember therefore from whence thou art fallen, and repent, and do the first works; or else I will come unto thee quickly, and will remove thy candlestick out of his place, except thou repent" (Rev. 2:2-5).

"Notice Christ's approach. He began by focusing on the good; the Ephesians' hard work, perseverance, and wise testing of the Apostles. First, he affirmed them for what they were doing right. Then having assured them, Christ turned to their need for change. You have forsaken your first love. Remember the height from which you have fallen!"[8]

At the point of rebuke the offender needs to know for certain he is not all trash, but that he is precious to you, and that you value his friendship. The offender needs to know you are not throwing him out and closing your door to the relationship. Reach out and affirm him with love, acceptance, and forgiveness.

"A recent survey in Albuquerque, New Mexico, revealed that one-out-of-five court suits has a Christian taking another Christian to court."[9] That is not the Christian way. Jesus taught a better way, the pathway of restoration and reconciliation.

Chapter 9

Making Wrongs Right

"Conflict simply IS! It can turn into painful or disastrous ends, but it doesn't need to. How we work through our differences, to a large extent, determines our whole life pattern."[1]

"... Determines our whole life pattern ...." How shockingly true! The way we work through conflict affects all areas of our life.

In order that we may gain victory over our blind spots, Jesus instructed His followers to practice one on one disciplining. How should the offender respond when he is approached about being wrong? How can wrongs be made right, and the damage done to another repaired? Going to the offender is only half of the project. The response of the offender is the other half. We teach the importance of *going* to the one who has committed the wrong, but little emphasis is placed on how to respond to or receive rebuke. The teachings of Jesus will become alive and meaningful if we respond properly. The approach is important; the proper response is equally important.

Linda was furious with her boss, Dr. Fenton. He had left without telling her how long he would be gone, or where he could be reached in case of an emergency. During his absence, Linda began to talk behind Dr. Fenton's back. She happened to know that he wasn't getting along with his wife, and she told some of her co-workers (confidentially, of course) that divorce was imminent. When Dr. Fenton returned a week later, he caught wind of the rumors and traced them to Linda.[2]

Two people need to do some repairing! The doctor needs to admit failure for not talking when he should have, and Linda for talking when she should not have. How do they repair the broken relationship?

Suppose a friend takes you out for breakfast. Your relationship is already strained. During the course of the meal, your friend makes it clear that because of your actions, he felt betrayed. Now what?

Your friend sends you signals of hurts, struggles, and pain, and wants you to listen. How should you respond? What is your responsibility?

Your brother takes you aside and explains to you that your present lifestyle is destroying the family. What are you going to do now?

Your uncle tries to help you understand that cold-shouldering your husband's mother is leaving her heartbroken and sick. How should you respond?

The community knows there is trouble in your marriage. Two brothers from your local congregation come to visit with you, and point out faults on your side. What should your response be?

Your mother tries to talk to you about the offensive music you listen to. Your father attempts to discuss your driving habits, and your grandfather is hurt by your sloppy, faddish dress. How will you react?

How does the Bible teach us to respond to corrective criticism, and make amends for wrongs we have done?

1. Do not be defensive.

Some people will basically never change. Thank God for the many believers who truly desire to follow the teachings of Jesus and help other Christians grow. But others have closed their door. They are not willing to break down the defensive barriers they have built. It would seem the offender is wallowing in his own cesspools with signs posted: "Leave me alone to die in this mess."

President Jefferson was riding horseback with some companions, and they came to a swollen stream. A foot traveler was there by the stream, waiting to ask someone on horseback to give him a ride across the rushing water. The president responded to the man's request. He pulled the man up on his horse, and later set him down on the opposite bank.

"Tell me," asked one of the men, "why did you ask the president to help you across?"

The man answered, "I didn't know he was the president. All I know is that on some faces is written the answer 'no' and on some faces is written the answer 'yes.' He had a yes face."[3]

The reason some people won't ever change some of their offensive behavior is that they are wearing a "no" face. Their defenses are etched all over their face. Their acquaintances know there is no point in making an approach.

The United States government has an enormous defense budget. The armed forces are ready to fight for this country in a moment's notice. The concept that a strong defense brings peace is erroneous. It is not accurate. A strong defense may ward off a serious fight, but it does not bring peace. Absence of fighting is not peace. Believers erroneously have their own built-in defense department. They stand ready to defend themselves at a moments notice. They even defend their pet sins whenever someone confronts them with their wrongs.

At one time in my life I nurtured the defense department more than the peacekeeping spirit. I entertained such attitudes as "He better clean up his own life before he says anything to me." God has shown me this is wrong.

Defense attitudes say, "Just let him say a word about it to me. I'm ready for him. I'll tell him to mind his own business." "I'll remind him of the wild stories I heard about him when he was young." "I'll let him know I'm no more in the wrong than he is, and he better repent first." "She sticks her nose into everyone's business, she better not bother me."

These attitude do not establish peace, but rather foster fights. Attitudes like these come naturally. We do not pray for them, or attend seminars on developing them. They are a part of our carnal nature, and need to be broken down by the work of the Holy Spirit in our lives.

One of the characteristics of a maturing, Spirit-led believer is that he or she is a teachable person, open for instruction.

"The fear of the Lord is the beginning of knowledge: but fools despise wisdom and instruction" (Prov. 1:7).

"He that refuseth instruction despiseth his own soul: but he that heareth reproof getteth understanding" (Prov. 15:32).

How should you respond to correction? Break down your defense department, and be open to instruction.

2. Listen!

"Wherefore, my beloved brethren, let every man be swift to hear, slow to speak, slow to wrath: For the wrath of man worketh not the righteousness of God" (James 1:19-20).

It isn't without design that God gave us two ears. His design is consistent with His Word, "Be swift to hear." "Let every man be quick to hear, (a ready listener)" (AMP).

Listen! Listen until you can feel the other's "hurt beat." When someone asks for your attention, *listen!* It may be urgent. The other individual may be hurting as a result of your wrong! You may say, "But that person has something against me!" That may be true. But if you do not listen until you feel the "hurt beat," you will not be able to make corrections. Listen until you have heard and felt the hurt.

We have excuses for not listening. "It is none of my business." That is not true! If you are part of the body of Christ, it is the responsibility of the hand to be aware of the needs of the foot. It is required of each member to undergird the other members whenever needed.

Or we may say, "But I'm no worse than . . . ." That may be true. But that does not relieve you of your responsibility toward God. It does not build Christian character. It develops in you the image of other sinners instead of Christ's image.

Others say, "I don't have time." This standard cop-out is an underhanded way of saying, "I really don't care how you feel about this situation. I want my own thing."

Listening is discerning and learning.

Author after author stress the importance of a listening ear.

John W. Drakeford wrote an entire book entitled *The Awesome Power of the Listening Ear* on this subject. He wrote, "He who would establish good relationships with people must learn to listen to them."[4]

Ray Stedman wrote, "The gift of a listening ear and an understanding heart is sometimes the greatest gift one Christian can give another."[5]

Alan Loy McGinnis emphasizes the therapy of listening:

> Patients come to psychiatric clinics like ours because they know so few people who will genuinely listen to them.
>
> When a woman announced that she was in analysis, a church-going friend admonished her; "You have Christian friends. If you have problems, why can't you talk to them?"
>
> "Well," she answered, "that would probably be all I'd need if one of them would really listen to me. But do you have any idea how quickly my church friends tune me out, and begin talking about themselves? It's embarrassing to have to pay for it, but to have someone give me 50 minutes of undivided attention does me a world of good."[6]

Richard Strauss' point should not be passed by! "Listening is hard work. Some people speak so slowly we want to drag their words out of them. We think five times faster than the average person can speak, and that intensifies the problem of listening. Others speak so rapidly that they run their words together and we cannot understand them. Some speak so softly we can't hear them. Others speak so loudly we are embarrassed to be near them. Some talk about things that are irrelevant or illogical. Others drone on about trivial and insignificant matters that bore us. Some can't seem to say what they mean. Others don't know when to wrap it up. All in all, listening can be a drag.

"But those very people who are most difficult to listen to may be the ones who most need a listener."[7]

Vance Havner challenges the people in the pews, "Everybody expects the preacher to be ready to preach, but who thinks of the congregation's responsibility to be ready to listen."[8]

The point is; when a hurting person comes to you, *listen!* It may be your faults that are causing the hurt. Listening may be a step toward healing and growth for both of you. The greatest Teacher of all said, "He that hath ears to hear, let him hear" (Matt: 11:15).

3. Admit the wrong.

After David *listened* to Nathan's story, and heard the words, "Thou art the man," he responded by saying, "I have sinned." The prodigal son returned to his father and said, "I have sinned."

It is not easy to say, "I have sinned," "I have wronged you," or, "I have hurt you." When we say and mean these words, they begin the healing process in our relationships. Too often we take the opposite way, the more natural route of excuses. We say, "I had the right intentions," "I'm not responsible for the whole thing," or, "The other person is more to blame than I am." "More times than not; however, our intentions are beside the point. We often harm others without specifically intending to harm them, yet our behavior is no less wrong."[9]

If I come rushing into the house to pick up my wallet in order to hurry to the hardware store before it closes, and vent my anger at my wife as I rush through, I have done wrong, whether I intended to or not.

The wife who snaps at her husband because the children have been on her nerves all day doesn't usually mean to vent her frustrations on him. While the circumstances of the day may make her behavior more understandable, they don't necessarily excuse her. If she is preoccupied with the question, "Did I really mean to snap at him?" without asking the more important one, "Was it wrong for me to snap at him?" her wrongdoing is not likely to be repaired.[10]

The real question is, did I wrong or hurt the other? If so, admit it. Let's suppose you and a friend have an accident on the corner of Fourth and Main streets. Your friend has a broken leg, and is bleeding from other cuts and bruises. You argue with him and make your point, you had the right-of-way. You may tell him it was his fault, then go on your way, leaving him wounded. He will admit you are right, but that does not bring healing, or stop the pain.

Simply explaining why you did certain things that hurt others does not repair the damage. Explaining your good intentions does not heal a broken heart. If you have hurt someone, even if you did have the right-of-way, healing needs to take place. It can happen when you humble yourself and say, "I realize that I have hurt you."

In order to admit and repair the wrong we do, we must realize that we are personally responsible for it. We should be able to say, "I did it: I am responsible for it."[11]

Every person is responsible for his own actions and reactions. When these actions hurt others, the individual is responsible to assist in healing and repairing the hurt. It cannot be done if you refuse to admit you were wrong.

4. Repent and renounce it!

Admitting we are wrong is the diagnosis. The real work of repairing must follow.

If the oil light in your car comes on, it is a signal something is wrong. You will probably arrange to have it towed to the local garage to have the problem checked. They may check the oil pressure, and sure enough — no pressure. That is the diagnosis. Now the work begins!

The diagnosis leads to correction and repair of the problem. Once we have taken the difficult step and admitted we were wrong; then we need to take the next step and repent and renounce it. To repent and renounce something is to choose that we no longer want any part of that sin. It is a decision we make. We decide to renounce the sin and wrongdoing that was hurting others. Too often we are attached to our wrongs. That is why a decision of repenting and renouncing the problem is needed. Some of our wrongs seem like fun and pleasure — we enjoy them. A person can know that an action is wrong, openly admit it, and yet not make a change in behavior. The missing element is a willingness to renounce the wrongdoing.

Ken Wilson's experience illustrates the point well. "I remember vividly an occasion when I had tremendous difficulty renouncing wrongdoing even though I had admitted that I was in the wrong. I used to be critical of other Christians. Before becoming a member of the Christian community to which I now belong, I met with one of the leaders to tell them what I didn't like about the group. In retrospect, I realize that some of my criticisms were fair, while others were not. But even if my criticisms were legitimate, my attitude was off."

The man he was sharing with told him, "Ken, you're coming into this with a critical spirit. And that is the wrong way for you to relate to brothers and sisters in Christ. I don't think you are going to be in a position to help us to improve unless you give up this attitude."

Ken had no problem admitting his attitude was wrong. He realized for the first time that God wanted him to give up that bad attitude. As he chose to respond in obedience to God, he experienced a fierce inner struggle. Finally he prayed, "Lord, I don't want to hold on to my critical spirit. I know it is wrong, and I renounce it! I don't want any part of it."[12]

For years Ken realized and recognized that he was too critical of others, but nothing changed until he took the important step of renouncing and repenting of his sin.

Notice the steps Ken took in renouncing his sin.

1. He verbalized it. He did not just think to himself, "I should quit that." He made a concrete statement, "Lord, I don't want to hold on to my critical spirit."

2. He stated *decisively* that something was actually wrong. He did not try to avoid the issue by saying, "Maybe I have a problem of being overly critical."

3. He was specific. It was clear what he was renouncing.

4. He was vigorous. He was struggling with giving up a fault he rather liked. He renounced it pointedly and with vigor. Jesus said, "Wherefore if thy hand or thy foot offend thee, cut them off, and cast them from thee: it is better for thee to enter into life halt or maimed, rather than having two hands or two feet to be cast into everlasting fire. And if thine eye offend thee, pluck it out, and cast it from thee: it is better for thee to enter into life with one eye, rather than having two eyes to be cast into hell fire" (Matt. 18:8-9).

Jesus is pointing out that wrongdoing is so serious that when it occurs, we must do whatever is necessary to renounce it. Peter sinned when he denied Christ. Yet his grief led to *repentance* and *reconciliation* with Jesus and the other disciples. He is an example for us to follow!

5. Then comes reconciliation!

Reconciliation means restoring the relationship. After you have repented of the wrong, go to the person you have wronged, and confess your sin.

Jesus said, "Therefore if thou bring thy gift to the altar, and there rememberest that thy brother hath ought against thee; Leave there thy gift before the altar, and go thy way; first be reconciled to thy brother, and then come and offer thy gift" (Matt. 5:23-24).

James wrote, "Confess your faults one to another, and pray one for another, that ye may be healed. The effectual fervent prayer of a righteous man availeth much" (James 5:16).

Inner emotions are healed as a result of fervent confession. Remember, in confession you are seeking reconciliation. So get to the point, don't hem and haw around. Do not say, "If I hurt you," as though that were a near impossibility, but confess your wrong!

May I point out that it was partly his fault? I was only part of the problem. *No you may not!* Your purpose is to make right your wrongs. Keep that goal in view, and do not cloud it with fault-slinging.

Reconciliation attitudes say, "I realize that what I did was wrong." "I realize my actions have hurt you." "I realize my critical spirit has made life difficult for you." "I realize my cold shoulder actions have caused you to feel rejected."

Identify the wrong you want repaired! Then say, "I am sorry," and seek forgiveness.

Ken Wilson again makes a significant point. "When you ask for forgiveness, be explicit. Say, 'Will you forgive me?' While this sounds simple enough, most Christians don't do it this way. Even when people go to the trouble of trying to be reconciled directly, the issue of forgiveness is rarely handled in a direct way. Instead, forgiveness is assumed, glossed over, forgotten, or bypassed."[13]

Sometimes years after an incident has transpired, the hurt pops up again when one or the other thought it was corrected. It could be that the incident was only explained away; you may have explained why you did it, and that it was his fault as much as yours. You may not have specifically asked, "Will you forgive me?" A specific request gives the other person an opportunity to give a specific response, "I forgive you."

All of this takes humility. But remember that humility is a basic ingredient in developing a Christlike character. When we admit wrongdoing, either to the Lord or to the person we've wronged, we are assuming a position of lowliness. To go to a friend and say, "Look, I was wrong when I talked to you the way I did the other day," is literally a humbling experience. It is the kind of experience that pride resists tooth and nail, but which Christlike humility urges us to embrace.[14]

Our response to Christ's teachings on correcting wrongs is important. If the principle is to work today, both approach and response must be correct.

A manager of a fast-food store urged the employee working at the counter to act friendly. But the boy continued treating the customers with little or no courtesy.

So, the manager stated his request a bit stronger: "Son, you really must be more friendly to customers." And this time he noticed a very slight improvement in the lad's manners, but it wasn't enough yet.

Finally the manager demanded, "You've got to act friendly!"

Promptly, almost angrily, the young man shot back, "I am friendly! They just can't see it."

But the manager was right; the boys actions spoke much louder than his words.[15]

So it is with many of us. We think we are right and friendly. Yet we fail to express the right attitudes when we make corrections.

Lay down the defenses, listen, own up to your wrongs, repent and renounce them, and confess and seek forgiveness. This is applying the oil of the Holy Spirit in our relationships. This builds Christian maturity in our lives, and develops meaningful relationships with each other.

Chapter 10

Oil of Forgiveness

Forgiving quickly is essential for joyful living and healthy relationships. Forgiving is something each of us must do often. It is usually not easy, and is never our natural response. It is almost impossible because it is contrary to the human nature that cries out for vengeance and judgment against the one who hurt you.

On the other hand, it is a necessity. If we do not forgive, we will be forced to live in a cage of resentment and bitterness that becomes smaller and stinkier with time until it crushes us and rots away all the joy and fulfillment of life.

Forgiveness is the oil of the Holy Spirit in a relationship. It makes things go smoothly. In contrast, an unforgiving attitude is Satanic sand in our relationship bearings that will destroy our "getting along" fellowship with each other and with God.

We will view forgiveness from three perspectives: God, the example; principles of forgiveness; and the command to forgive.

1. God, the example of forgiveness.

"For thou, Lord, art good, and ready to forgive; and plenteous in mercy unto all them that call upon thee. But thou, O Lord, art a God full of compassion, and gracious, longsuffering, and plenteous in mercy and truth" (Ps. 86:5,15).

The psalmist David is emphasizing that God is one who is ready to forgive. God is ready to spare and pardon the offender.

"The Lord is merciful and gracious, slow to anger, and

plenteous in mercy. He will not always chide: neither will he keep his anger for ever. He hath not dealt with us after our sins; nor rewarded us according to our iniquities. For as the heaven is high above the earth, so great is his mercy toward them that fear him. As far as the east is from the west, so far hath he removed our transgressions from us. Like as a father pitieth his children, so the Lord pitieth them that fear him. For he knoweth our frame; he remembereth that we are dust. As for man, his days are as grass: as a flower of the field, so he flourisheth. For the wind passeth over it, and it is gone; and the place thereof shall know it no more. But the mercy of the Lord is from everlasting to everlasting upon them that fear him, and his righteousness unto children's children; To such as keep his covenant, and to those that remember his commandments to do them" (Ps. 103:8-18).

This is another Psalm of David written soon after Nathan confronted him concerning his sins of adultery and murder.

Nathan told David, ". . . The Lord also hath put away thy sin; thou shalt not die" (2 Sam. 12:13). David experienced the abundance of God's forgiveness. According to the Old Testament law, David should have been stoned to death. Instead, God granted him mercy and forgiveness. In the Psalms David exclaims, "The Lord is merciful and gracious . . . He will not always chide . . . He hath not dealt with us after our sins . . . As far as the east is from the west, so far hath he removed our transgressions from us" (Ps. 103:8-12).

Notice that David did not say north and south. I am glad he did not; because if you travel due north until you reach the north pole, you cannot travel north any further. You can only go south. There are limits to the extent that we can travel north or south. However, if you travel due east, you can *never, never,* come to the end of east. There is no east pole, there are no limits to traveling east. "There is no limit to eastness."[1]

David tells us from personal experience of the wonder of God's forgiveness. There are no limits to God's forgiveness.

"And in Him you have been made complete, and He is the head over all rule and authority. . . having been buried with Him in baptism, in which you were also raised up with Him through faith in the working of God, who raised Him from the dead. And when you were dead in your transgressions and the uncircumcision of your flesh, He made you alive together with Him, having forgiven us all our transgressions, having canceled out the certificate of debt consisting of decrees against us and which was hostile to us; and He has taken it out of the way, having nailed it to the cross" (Col. 2:10,12-14;NAS).

"Having forgiven us our transgressions." What does this mean? To grant as a favor, gratuitously, in kindness, pardon and rescue, deliver, freely give and grant, (frankly) forgive. This is God's example of forgiveness.

"Then said Jesus, Father, forgive them; for they know not what they do. And they parted his raiment, and cast lots" (Luke 23:34). Jesus was forgiving His enemies, even as they were driving the nails into His hands, and leaving Him to hang on the cross. While being crucified and under the curse of His enemies' anger, He cried to the Father to forgive (to lay aside, omit) them, because they did not know what they were doing.

God's readiness to forgive was demonstrated by Jesus Christ at the Last Supper in the Upper Room. There was one in the room who would betray Him. Jesus dips the bread, and serves Judas first. "Judas is the first to receive food, a sign of honor. This is love's last appeal! Jesus is reaching out to him as a friend. It must have been a long, intense moment of struggle when Jesus gave Judas the bread."[2]

Jesus reached out to Judas! If only Judas would have just pushed his fingers a few inches further, taken hold of Jesus' hand, pulled himself into the bosom of Jesus and cried "Lord, forgive!" he too could have experienced the mercy of God. Jesus showed that God is ready to forgive.

God is the example of forgiveness. He is ready to forgive, full of compassion, and plenteous in mercy. There is no east pole, there are no limits to God's forgiveness.

2. Principles of forgiveness.

"Giving thanks unto the Father, which hath made us meet to be partakers of the inheritance of the saints in light: Who hath delivered us from the power of darkness, and hath translated us into the kingdom of his dear Son: In whom we have redemption through his blood, even the forgiveness of sins" (Col. 1:12-14).

We were under the domination of the devil, bound by the power of darkness, and deserving the judgment of God; but we received forgiveness. Because of God's forgiveness, we were translated from the realm of darkness into the kingdom of Jesus Christ. We received a gift!

"In whom we have redemption through his blood, the forgiveness of sins, according to the riches of his grace" (Eph. 1:7).

"In whom we have redemption . . . ." We were kidnapped slaves. Jesus came to our rescue, and paid our ransom. He paid it fully and completely with His blood. He bought us back. He set us free. *He forgave us!* He now reckons us as His sons, as though we had *never* sinned.

Especially notice two principles of forgiveness in these verses. First, forgiveness is a gift from God. It cannot be purchased or earned by any man. Secondly, we cannot keep it to ourselves, we must pass it on.

"And forgive us our debts, as we forgive our debtors. And lead us not into temptation, but deliver us from evil: For thine is the kingdom, and the power, and the glory, for ever. Amen. For if ye forgive men their trespasses, your heavenly Father will also forgive you" (Matt. 6:12-14).

Forgiveness is a gift. We *cannot* experience it without passing it on to those around us.

"And when ye stand praying, forgive, if ye have ought against any: that your Father also which is in heaven may forgive you your trespasses. But if ye do not forgive, neither will your Father which is in heaven forgive your trespasses" (Mark 11:25-26).

3. Commands to forgive.

Jesus said, "Judge not, and ye shall not be judged: condemn not, and ye shall not be condemned: forgive, and ye shall be forgiven" (Luke 6:37).

The Greek word translated forgiveness in this verse is a strong and forceful word. It means release, relieve, dismiss, to free fully, let go, loose, put at liberty. "To forgive in real life means dropping the charges against the other."[3]

We were scoundrels and sinners, but God loved us, and

dropped the charges against us because of the atoning work of Jesus Christ. Whatever our gripe may be against another, regardless of the hurt we may have felt, forgiveness means we drop the charges of guilt pressed against the offender.

Whenever we have been wronged, we generally place demands on the guilty individual. You must come to me in tears before I can forgive. You must change your behavior. You must pay me back double, you must repair what you broke. These are demands! *Forgiveness means canceling demands!* When the prodigal son returned home to his father, his father was not waiting with a list of demands. They were canceled! He was ready to receive his son into his bosom. Many people are distant in their relationships, because they will not pay the cost of canceling demands. Husbands and wives divorce, and live in separate houses because they simply cannot cancel demands.

"On the other hand, forgiveness is not mere toleration, or just putting up with the other, or looking the other way. It is more than politeness, tact, or diplomacy. It is not suppressing or forgetting. It is the painful act of dropping charges even though you are wronged, and canceling the demands attached to the wrongs committed against you."[4]

"And be ye kind one to another, tenderhearted, forgiving one another, even as God for Christ's sake hath forgiven you" (Eph. 4:32).

"Forbearing one another, and forgiving one another, if any man have a quarrel against any: even as Christ forgave you, so also do ye" (Col. 3:13).

As we look at the context of Scriptures addressing forgiveness, we notice some of the elements of unforgiveness. Unforgiveness is somewhat like an egg. An egg consists of a shell, a yoke, and egg white. That equals an egg. Unforgiveness is also comprised of various ingredients. We find them listed in the Scripture in contrast to the forgiveness passages. In Ephesians 4:31, we find these elements of unforgiveness: bitterness, rage, anger, quarrelsome attitudes, slander, ill will, and spite. Colossians 3:13 says that if we have a quarrel or complaint against anyone, we are to forgive.

So — unforgiveness is a result of anger, resentment, bitterness, jealousy, and similar sins. On the other hand, notice the qualities of forgiveness: kindness, compassion, gentleness, humility, and patience.

Alan McGinnis wrote, "You can't be free and happy if you harbor grudges, so put them away. Get rid of them. Collect postage stamps, or collect coins, if you wish, but don't collect grudges."[5]

"... *Forgive*, and ye shall be forgiven" (Luke 6:37). If you do not forgive, you cannot be forgiven. Unforgiveness always carries with it the goal of getting even, of measuring and giving out revenge and judgment on the offender. *God strictly forbids that!*

How is it that God does not forgive us if we do not forgive others?

1. When God forgave us, we were given the cancellation of sin's penalties. We became a child of God. We were restored to close fellowship with God. Our relationship with God was put back in the position of righteousness.

What does it mean then to forgive another? It is no different than the forgiveness God has extended to us. If we say, "I forgive," but the relationship does not restore closeness, or a sense of normality; we have not forgiven. If the offended continues to punish the offender by withholding fellowship, pulling the shocks, and keeping him at arm's length, he has not forgiven.

I do not believe that God demands, with a rod in one hand, that if you do not forgive, "Neither will I forgive you of this or that sin." Rather, your unforgiveness is a roadblock that does not permit God's forgiveness to flow through to you.

Remember, *forgiveness from God means a restoration of a close spiritual relationship. Forgiveness of another means restoration of fellowship and friendship.*

The Bible teaches that if we do not love those whom we see, we do not love God whom we cannot see. Your love for God is equated with your love for others. Jesus taught that as we have done to the least of these, we have done unto Him.

This is the crux of the matter! Your fellowship with others is a sure indicator of the depth of your fellowship with God. Your closeness to God *cannot* exceed by very much your closeness to those around you. A son cannot have a wrong relationship with dad, and a good relationship with God.

If you are withholding forgiveness, fellowship and closeness from an offender, *you* are blocking off fellowship and closeness with God. You are blocking off your intimacy with His love and grace. The chip you carry on your shoulder wears you down, makes you nasty to be around, and hinders your walk of joy in the Lord.

"And forgive us our debts, as we forgive our debtors" (Matt. 6:12).

2. *Unforgiveness brings guilt upon us.*

Unforgiveness is produced from anger, resentment, bitterness, jealousy, and other such sins. Whenever a believer harbors these sins, he becomes guilty. A guilty person does not have the joy of the Lord. His expression and countenance look like he lost his best friend, and the whole world is down on him. Such attitudes make life miserable for others. Unforgivers are miserable with guilt. Their guilt and misery blocks out the joy of the Lord. That feeling of emptiness is not God shaking a stick at them and saying, "I won't forgive," it is a result of their unforgiving attitudes. It works like an umbrella, keeping that person from the joy of the Lord, release from guilt, and assurance of forgiveness.

Paul Faulkner made a good point about this. "Of course you can cling to your grudge if you want to. But when you do, you use your strength for this day making yourself and the people around you feel miserable and guilty. Or, you can cut the line to what is behind you through the power of forgiveness and use your strength to strain toward what lies ahead."[6]

We make it hard for others to forgive when we continue to express resentment, rudeness, unkindness, and bitterness in our relationships. It is sin — it causes others to stumble over our unforgiveness. Everything about unforgiveness is contrary to God, His nature, and His command to be kind one to another. Unforgiveness becomes an artesian well of misery. It drains the joy out of our life, and lets the misery flow to others.

In the Lord's Prayer, Jesus taught us to pray, ". . . and forgive us our debts, as we forgive our debtors" (Matt. 6:12). "To forgive, as we forgive, is to recognize that God cannot renew those who stubbornly cling to grudges, thus defying His extension of grace."[7]

It is sin in the heart that prevents us from experiencing God's grace, and the inner joy of cleansing and forgiveness. It is impossible to be right on every count, and fail only in forgiveness. Unforgiveness is a result of sin in the heart. Unforgiveness is produced by anger, jealousy, resentment, hatred, or bitterness. One, or any combination of these sins in the heart will be enough to produce an unforgiving spirit.

Here is the recipe for a solid chunk of unforgiveness. Take a hurt or offense against you. Let it slowly stew on the front burner of your heart throughout the day. That evening, add anger and thoroughly stir until it colors the entire bowl of hurt. Flavor it with a cup of envy, and three heaping spoons of jealousy; mix thoroughly, and add a liberal pinch of resentment. After mixing it for the evening, slide it into the oven that is set at "hatred" and bake overnight. You will have a hard cake of unforgiveness ready for you the next morning.

Here is the point. Anger easily becomes unforgiveness. Hatred is an ingredient of unforgiveness. Jealousy can quickly be translated into unforgiveness. Selfishness is an appetizer for unforgiveness. Resentment is unforgiveness. Envy is unforgiving. Bitterness will not forgive.

These are sins of the heart: they are works of the flesh. The Bible pointedly states that ". . . they which do such things shall not inherit the kingdom of God" (Gal. 5:21). Unforgiveness by itself is not the root problem. When these uncleansed and unforgiven sins stand in the way, *we cannot forgive. These sins produce unforgiveness.* When unforgiveness is in our heart, it means we are continuing to wallow in the sins of the flesh. Until we are cleansed by the blood of Jesus, we will have a dirty sinful record. It is this dirty record that wards off God's joy in our life and produces unforgiveness.

To experience the blessing of God's forgiveness, we must repent of our jealousy, pride, anger, resentment, and bitterness. Oswald Chambers wrote, "God cannot forgive a man unless he repents."[8] God cannot forgive you if you refuse to seek His cleansing and forgiveness for these sins.

The Bible says in Ephesians 4:31, "put away" these sins. It

means to clean up your life, put these sins away, and put on kindness. In the repenting process, you take on humility. Then forgiveness is ready to burst into blossom. Jesus illustrated this principle in the parable of the unmerciful servant.

"Then Peter came up to Him and said, Lord, how many times may my brother sin against me, and I forgive him and let him go? As many as up to seven times? Jesus answered him, I tell you, not up to seven times, but seventy times seven! Therefore the kingdom of heaven is like a human king who wished to settle accounts with his attendants. When he began accounting, one was brought to him who owed him ten thousand talents (probably about $10,000,000.00), And because he could not pay, his master ordered him to be sold, with his wife and his children and everything that he possessed, and payment to be made. So the attendant fell on his knees, begging him, Have patience with me and I will pay you everything. And his master's heart was moved with compassion, and he released him and forgave him (canceling) the debt. But that same attendant, as he went out, found one of his fellow attendants who owed him a hundred denarii (about $20.00); and he caught him by the throat and said, Pay what you owe! So his fellow attendant fell down and begged him earnestly, Give me time, and I will pay you all! But he was unwilling and went out and had him put in prison till he should pay the debt. When his fellow attendants saw what had happened, they were greatly distressed, and they went and told everything that had taken place to their master. Then his master called him and said to him, You contemptible and wicked attendant! I forgave and canceled all that (great) debt of yours because you begged me; And should you not have had pity and mercy on your fellow attendant, as I had pity and mercy on you? And in wrath his master turned him over to the torturers (the jailers), till he should pay all that he owed. So also My heavenly Father will deal with every one of you, if you do not freely forgive your brother from your heart his offenses" (Matt. 18:21-35;AMP).

This attendant owed the king a huge, *unpayable* debt. The king commanded that he, his family, and his belongings were to be sold. The attendant prostrated himself before the king begging for patience.

The king was so moved with pity and compassion that he canceled the debt, forgave him, and set him free. This particular attendant had *not* realized what the king had done for him. His heart was so filled with selfishness that he completely missed having a heart of mercy. He was so preoccupied in looking out for himself that he stumbled over his own sins. As a result of his selfishness, the king said to him, "And should you not have had pity and mercy on your fellow attendant as I had pity and mercy on you?"

God wants us to have the same attitude of heart toward others as He has toward us. We cannot experience mercy and compassion, which translates into forgiveness, when there is selfishness, envy, and jealousy in our hearts.

Who is Hurt Because of Unforgiveness?

Keep in mind that unforgiveness grows out of other sins in the heart. Who are the real losers when unforgiveness rules in people's lives? Actually, everyone. In the parable of the unmerciful servant, everyone involved lost. The king lost an attendant, and a working relationship with the man. The family lost by having him in prison, but the big loser was the attendant himself.

Anna had been sitting motionless for hours. She did not touch her meal. She just sat and stared blankly into space. Dr. Wilson walked by and said, "Hi, Anna." Anna did not respond. In fact, she had not responded for years. Anna is in a mental hospital. She has not spoken since she entered 12 years ago. Could Anna speak if she wanted to? She has the vocal cords. But she doesn't want to speak. She hasn't spoken since she broke up with her fiancé. What can make a person strong enough not to speak to anyone for 12 years? Anger can!"[9]

Because of anger, she cannot forgive. She has destroyed her own life. Her life is miserable, not only to herself, but also to those around her.

Let's take a look at what happens to this couple we will call John and Sue. Their marriage is off to a very romantic start. It has all the makings of a successful marriage. Children are added to the family, and no one suspects any serious problems. Years go by, and the frustrations begin to leak to friends and neighbors. The husband's behavior lacks some of the finer qualities of the Christian life. The wife now becomes angry about some of her husband's actions.

They are able to see the other's faults much quicker than their own. They try to prove that the other is the real problem in the marriage. In their strained relationship, they take stabs at each other in attempts to prove the other wrong. Things turn sour and bitter. Forgiveness is not even peeking over the horizon. Their marriage becomes a battleground of getting even with each other. Who loses?

Ray is a man who recognized his sin. He confessed it to God and received his forgiveness. He confessed it to those whom he wronged. He longs for a close and restored relationship. Instead, the other puts more distance between them: he refuses to forgive! Who loses?

I have a minister friend who has several habitual critics in the congregation where he pastors. They freely inform him of his wrongs. Sure, he has made some mistakes, but he has done what he knows to do to regain fellowship. They continue to hold him at double arm's length. This is a huge burden on this man's ministry. His heart bleeds to be forgiven. Who loses?

It is true that the person who refuses to forgive is the biggest loser. But to say that the offended is hurting himself, and not me, is a lie. Sometimes we hear the self-righteous, pious remark "He is not hurting me." That is far from the truth. If you do not forgive me to the extent that we can enjoy lunch together again, *I'm hurting*. It affects me. It affects my spiritual life.

When couples refuse to forgive, they destroy their own relationship, and hurt those around them. Unforgiveness hurts everyone involved. It hurts the children, and changes their course of life. It hurts the grandparents, and brings tension to the family gatherings. It hurts the neighbors, and sets them one against the other. It becomes a plague to the Church, and puts an ugly stigma on the body of Christ. It is a victory for the devil, and a defeat to the Church. It is like poison ivy; it hurts where it touches, with no one immune from its sting.

Dwight L. Carlson wrote, "Forgiveness is giving up my right to hurt back if you hurt me."[10]

Those who refuse to forgive continue to try to hit back at those who hurt them. In the process, they hurt themselves and those with whom they come in contact. Eventually, people who harbor unforgiveness develop an arrogant, adamant, bitter, and hard-hearted attitude toward the person whom they despise. *That soon becomes that person's personality.* It is not by mere chance that there are hard-hearted people hurting friends and strangers alike as they bully their way down the lane of life. Unforgiveness produces *contemptible* personalities. Those who do not forgive suffer immensely. So do those around them.

When people don't forgive —
1. They are led by their anger, pain, or hatred;
2. They are directed by negative memories;
3. They do not act freely;
4. They try to keep a controlling grasp on situations and people;
5. They are pressured by lives of tension and stress;
6. They probably shorten their lives;
7. Their relationships with others are strained;
8. Their relationship with God is weakened;
9. They live with feelings of little self-worth;
10. They feel unrelieved guilt.[11]

How Often Shall We Forgive?

You have heard it said again and again, "I've had it! I can't take it any longer! I've just got to get out!"

Jesus said, "Take heed to yourselves: If thy brother trespass against thee, rebuke him; and if he repent, forgive him. And if he trespass against thee seven times in a day, and seven times in a day turn again to thee, saying, I repent; thou shalt forgive him" (Luke 17:3-4).

If someone offends or hurts you seven times in one day, and he asks you to forgive him that often, Jesus says *forgive him!* Can you imagine someone squashing your toes, and then saying, "I'm sorry, please forgive me"? You reply, "Yes, I forgive." Then it happens again! This time you may say, "I am still hurting from the first time, yes, I'll forgive, but don't do it again." But seven times a day! Most of us would not make it past the third offense.

"Then came Peter to him, and said, Lord, how oft shall my brother sin against me, and I forgive him? till seven times? Jesus saith unto him, I say not unto thee, Until seven times: but Until seventy times seven" (Matt. 18:21-22).

Peter asked Jesus if forgiving seven times is enough. Jesus multiplied the seven by seventy, and made it 490 times.

How could anyone sin against me 490 times a day and need forgiveness? That means he would have to sin every three minutes, 24 hours a day. *That calls for a continual forgiving spirit.* No one sins against you that often. But you may need to forgive that much.

"A wrongdoing inflicting deep hurt is not forgiven and then forgotten in a moment. The pain of hurt and resentment hits way down deep inside the very heart of one's nerve center. The sights of things, recollection of events, remarks of others — all these keep reminding you that you've been wronged. So forgive — 490 times a day if necessary. Forgive 490 times if the deep temptation and pain of retaliation returns that often. Forgiveness continues as often as the reminder of the deed and hurt return."[12]

My brother experienced a deep hurt and disappointment. He felt he was wronged and carried a grudge and burden against the offender for years. He became deadlocked with his feelings. He couldn't escape the feelings of revenge, anger, and disappointment because of the way he was treated. People with good intentions advised him to just forgive and forget. However; the hurt was so deeply inflicted, and the pain so keenly felt that forgetting was not even possible. If forgetting is not possible, how can he forgive?

"It doesn't mean to just forget. It means to drop all charges against the other. It means to cancel all the angry demands of restitution required from the other person."[13]

That is not, however; the end of the matter. A person who has been hurt deeply, and the pain has worn him down over the years, cannot by one simple prayer restore and heal the entire relationship. When he sees that person again, the hurt returns again and again and again.

My brother wanted to forgive from his heart. However;

handling the recurring pain and continuing to forgive a remembered offense was another matter. We approached it from this angle: when you are out in the field plowing, and you come to the end of the field, if you look across the road, you will see the offender working by his barn. The pain of hurt and resentment returns to hit you in the stomach. Now what do you do? Forgive again! Drop the charges! Cancel the demands! Do it every time you plow around that field, even if it is 490 times.

My brother chose to forgive. At that point, healing began to transpire. Then the grace of God flooded over him, giving him the ability to forgive, and the joy of God entered his life.

When Do You Need to Forgive?

Richard Walters listed several questions that are helpful in pointing out our need to forgive and be free:

> The questions on the list below will help make us aware of our need to forgive someone. Any of these items can be related to other matters; but when we become aware of these attitudes or actions in ourselves, we should determine if, perhaps, we have been hurt by someone and have neglected to forgive that person for the offense.
>
> 1. Do I think often about the hurt? (This is the seed bed for resentment.)
> 2. When I think of the hurt, do I have strong feelings of anger?
> 3. Do I imagine difficulty or injury coming to the person who hurt me?
> 4. Do I avoid the person or not communicate with him or her when it would be easy for me to do so?
> 5. Do I have physical symptoms of tension, tightness, stomach disorder, or insomnia?
> 6. Am I irritable? Do I easily get angry about little things?
> 7. Do I indirectly attack the other person? This might take the form of hostile humor, spreading half true stories, trying to turn children or others against

that person, failing to cooperate or be supportive, or any of hundreds of other forms of passive — aggressive behavior.

8. Do I attack the person directly through harsh insults, sarcasm, physical attack, withholding child support payments, or some other form of direct attack?

9. Am I highly critical of myself? Am I discontented with life, self demanding, self condemning, or generally dissatisfied with myself?

If our answers to items 7 or 8 above, and perhaps others, are yes, it is our responsibility to change our behavior, and to apologize for our sins against the other person as well as to forgive. In every instance when we forgive someone else, we need to pray that God will make us aware of our sins against the other person. We must also pray for humility and charity in our relationships.[14]

Suppose You Don't Feel Like Forgiving

Remember and ponder this: there really is no other option for the believer. We are commanded to forgive — not by the person who wronged us, but by the Lord himself. Our willingness to forgive others is connected to our receiving God's forgiveness. "Forgive us our trespasses as we forgive those who trespass against us."[15]

Remember this also. Forgiveness is an act of the will. It is a choice we make. It is not a feeling by itself. My brother made a choice to forgive. After he chose to do so, he began feeling better.

Forgiveness is our action toward the other person, based on a decision not to hold the wrong against them. We can choose to forgive even when our feelings are saying, no, never.[16]

Sometimes our feelings of resentment are so strong that we need to ask the offender for time to deal with our own anger, and give it time to cool off. When we have had time to deal with our own sins, we must then go back to the individual, and affirm our forgiveness.

Don't Miss This Principle

There are three important phrases that are often like foreign language to the believer. 1. I'm sorry I hurt you or wronged you. 2. Will you forgive me? 3. I forgive you!

Just as we ask God for forgiveness, we need to ask others to forgive us. That makes a *reference point* for restoring the relationship. In return, it is important to say, "I forgive you." When these two aspects are present, relationships are quickly restored. If they are not part of our walk of life, our relationships will remain strained.

A stockbroker, whom I will call George, tells of having a falling out with another broker in the same office. They had a dispute over a customer, and after that, they did not speak. One day in church, as George was praying the Lord's Prayer, he came to that line on forgiveness. "There was no question in my mind," he says, "who was in the wrong. Sam had been in the wrong when he took my customer away from me. But it wasn't right for me not to be speaking, and I had to do something. While the others were repeating the rest of the prayer, I asked God to help me with Sam. On Monday afternoon, when the market had closed and I was finishing up some papers, I breathed another prayer and went over to Sam's desk and said, 'You know, Sam, you used to tell me about the trouble your wife was having with arthritis, and I've been wondering how she is getting along.'

"Sam looked startled at first, but then words began to tumble out — how they'd had her to three specialists in the past year, and that she was a little better, thank you. And as we talked he told me about taking a walk together for two blocks the night before, which was pretty good. And among other things, he said that he was too quick with his tongue and often did things he didn't mean to do. Though he didn't come out and say it, I knew it was Sam's way of apologizing.

"And the next morning when he came by my

desk, he said, just like he used to, 'Good morning, George!' And I said, just like I used to, 'Good morning, Sam!' "[17]

While this story lacks some of the biblical steps in making wrongs right, there is a very noteworthy aspect to it. They reached the desired goal in what forgiveness means — a restored relationship.

Tim LaHaye quotes a story that illustrates the point well. "Some missionaries for the Wycliffe Bible Translators were trying to translate the Bible into the Rincon dialect of the Mexican Zapotec Indians. When they came to the sentence, 'I forgive you,' they had a difficult time communicating the meaning to the Indians. To convey the sentence in a way that the Indians would understand, they finally translated it, 'My face heals toward you.' "[18]

These two stories illustrate what the end results of dropping charges and canceling demands should bring about. Restored relationships and healed faces.

Chapter 11

Me People
— We
People

Little Joey and Billy are playing on Grandma and Grandpa's living room floor. Grandpa is reclined in the easy chair, the newspaper in his lap, and a half expressed grin on his face. *It is nice to have such cute grandchildren,* he thinks to himself. Then, just before he dozes off one of them screams, "It's mine!"

Grandpa promptly corrects his grandchildren. They cannot grow up to be so selfish. An hour later their mother comes to get her children. As she is getting them dressed in their coats and caps, one of the little boys picks up a toy to take along home, and his brother promptly screams, "No, it's mine."

Dad gives his daughter some advice about his grandchildren. "We've got to get this selfish spirit out of them. They will grow up to be adult brats. Where did they ever learn to be so selfish?" Mamma gets her two boys quiet enough to kiss Grandma and Grandpa goodnight, and the three head toward home.

Grandpa watches as they get into the car and drive out of the lane. As the taillights slip away behind the hill, he heads for his chair. He gives Grandma a puzzled glance as he reaches for the newspaper.

He is dozing off as the evening's happenings roll through his mind. *We've got to get this selfish spirit out of them. We need to teach them to let the other have the biggest cookie, the first choice, and a chance at life. We've got to teach them how to play together. We can't tolerate their present conduct! It's embarrassing!*

His mind rambles on sleepily. He sees two brothers in a business deal where money is involved. The one brother thought it should be split 50/50; the other thought he should have a greater share. He had always secretly begrudged his brother after the payer had written them each a check for equal amounts.

From then on, his relationship with his brother was strained. He kept his distance from him, and found another job. As he awakes he is saying to himself, "Someone should have taught those two brothers something."

Then he remembers — as clear as day — *That was me 30 years ago. My brother and our families seldom see each other to this day.*

Grandpa dozes off. He recalls a committee meeting at work. Ideas are put out on the table. One man present had ideas all his own. He didn't want to hear the suggestions of the others, especially suggestions given by one couple he didn't care for. The couple's ideas carried, and the man lost his control over the situation.

Since he was no longer in control of planning the event, he and his wife dropped that particular couple out of their social activities, and held them at arm's length.

He awakes with a jolt! That can't be me! But it is. Ten years ago, we dropped our friends out of our lives because we could not control the event.

Grandpa sits and thinks. As his mind continues to wander, the clock strikes every 30 minutes, reminding him that his life is ". . . even a vapour, that appeareth for a little time, and then vanisheth away" (James 4:14).

He remembers a pastor trying to bring the congregation to a point of discerning the will of God. He saw the Church coming to a conclusion on the matter. One man in attendance that evening was very unhappy with the decision. He became angry, and left with a "huff and puff." He had grumbled to himself for weeks, and even occasionally snapped at his wife and children. In a "huff" he decided to leave that particular church, and find one with a more "spiritual atmosphere." There had been little contact with that group of people since that time.

He remembers vividly, I was that man! As he sees himself mirrored in his grandchildren, he stands to his feet and starts pacing the floor, as he ponders to himself, *You know, I have basically lived my life for ME. Now that I have it my way, I don't like it. It doesn't give me the inner satisfaction and peace I want. I really never gave up my life. Did I miss the real meaning of Jesus' words, "For whosoever will save his life shall lose it: and whosoever will lose his life for my sake shall find it"?* (Matt. 16:25).

I had a lot of things in life that were exclusively mine. Now, as I see myself in my grandchildren, I no longer feel free to enjoy what I thought was mine.

Just like grandpa in our story, so many believers experience deep struggles with others because they are basically looking out for Number One. They say, "I must look out for *ME.*" They never deal with their own selfishness. They have never placed the ME factor in submission to the absolute lordship of Jesus Christ.

It is possible for believers to experience a "holy limp," as I referred to earlier, and yet never continue cultivating brokenness as a *way of life* before God. It is possible to have a repentant attitude toward our own sinfulness, but then slip back and live for ME.

The Bible says, "If it is possible, as far as it depends on you, live at peace with everyone" (Rom. 12:18;NIV).

Our ability to live at peace with others depends largely on whether we are ME people, or WE people. A change in our heart attitudes goes a long way in cultivating close relationships.

Saul (Paul) was a ME person from the best stock of Israel. But he counted it all loss for the "... excellency of the knowledge of Christ Jesus my Lord..." (Phil. 3:8). He chose to become a WE person for the good of others. He said, "For though I be free from all men, yet have I made myself *servant* unto all, that I might gain the more" (1 Cor. 9:19).

Paul was willing to become a slave for the good of others, to become a servant to all people. Paul was a WE person. He entreated the Philippians to make his joy complete by being like-minded and ". . . having the same love, being of one accord, of one mind" (Phil. 2:2). He wanted them to maintain love, be united in one accord, and in one spirit and purpose. They were admonished to be WE people.

Then he drove the WE principle deeper. "Do nothing out of selfish ambition or vain conceit, but in humility consider others better than yourselves. Each of you should look not only to your own interests, but also to the interests of others" (Phil. 2:3-4;NIV). Here the Scripture instructs that we are not to act or react with vain conceit, selfish ambition, or strife, but rather respond with humility, regarding my brother as more important than myself. This is not easy, nor does it come naturally. We are to *look out* for the interests of our friends as well as ourselves. This develops WE people.

Our chief example is Jesus Christ. "Let this mind be in you, which was also in Christ Jesus" (Phil. 2:5). "Your attitude should be the same as that of Christ Jesus" (NIV).

What was His attitude? He came to be a servant. He became a slave, one who gave himself for others. He gave up His privileges and dignity to become a bond-servant. He became a WE person. We are called to the same walk of life.

You will recall when Jesus prayed in the Garden of Gethsemane, He pled with God, "Father, if thou be willing, remove this cup from me. . . ." As time progressed that eventful night, Jesus chose to submit himself to the will of His Father, even though it meant separation from His loving Father and death. He chose to fall on His face and pray, ". . . nevertheless not my will, but thine, be done" (Luke 22:42). Jesus laid down His request for release, so that WE might become children of God. He felt a restored relationship between God and man a greater necessity than what He would have desired for himself.

We like that good "inside" feeling we experience as a result of good relationships. Nothing that can compare with those close friendships where love, acceptance, and belonging is *felt*. We like the expression of the Psalmist, "Behold, how good and how pleasant it is for brethren to dwell together in unity!" (Ps. 133:1).

There is a cost for such beauty. It is the laying down of the

ME ambition. The oil that brings about such smooth relationships comes through following the biblical mandate of being WE persons.

Notice the clarity with which the Scriptures speak on the subject.

"Let us therefore follow after the things which make for peace, and things wherewith one may edify another" (Rom. 14:19).

"We then that are strong ought to bear the infirmities of the weak, and not to please ourselves. Let every one of us please his neighbor for his good to edification" (Rom. 15:1-2).

"Let no man seek his own, but every man another's wealth" (1 Cor. 10:24).

"Whether therefore ye eat, or drink, or whatsoever ye do, do all to the glory of God. Give none offense, neither to the Jews, nor to the Gentiles, nor to the church of God: Even as I please all men in all things, not seeking mine own profit, but the profit of many, that they may be saved" (1 Cor. 10:31-33).

"Doth not behave itself unseemly, seeketh not her own, is not easily provoked, thinketh no evil" (1 Cor. 13:5).

"Two are better than one . . . . For if they fall, the one will lift up his fellow . . ." (Eccles. 4:9-10).

Here is a test to help you discern for yourself whether you are a ME person, or whether you choose to live by WE principles.

ME people:
— Talk a lot about themselves in a conversation.
— Don't bother to check the feelings of those involved.
— Getting what they want is more important than how others may feel.
— Line out their turf, set the tune, and the rest of the folks better fit in.
— See others who do not fit their mold as a nuisance to be avoided.
— Push others back who don't play like they do.
— Inflict hurts and wounds that become relationship casualties.
— Justify their actions to avoid being wrong.

— Make justifications rather than corrections.
— Seldom confess or apologize for an offense.
— Must be in control to be involved.
— Refuse to play if they can not run the show.
— Do not maintain a close relationship with people they cannot control, even if that person is their own spouse.
— Are reckless about observing the organization's policies.
— Do not follow the Church's standard of practice.
— Respect authority only if the persons holding the office are nice.
— Do not see the beauty of accountability to one another.
— See their own actions as "none of your business."
— Do not want to be told what to do.

If any of these descriptions express your lifestyle, you need God's help! You are not doing your best to live at peace with all men. You may be missing the joy of close-knit friendships.

ME people are not well suited for leadership. The Bible says, "For the overseer must be above reproach as God's steward, not *self-willed*, not *quick-tempered*" (Titus 1:7;NAS).

This helps explain why some people who are given leadership positions seem to drive people away. They are basically self-willed: they are ME people.

History records gruesome accounts of ME people in authority. King Herod was one such man. When he heard that Jesus was born King of the Jews, he ordered all the children in Bethlehem two years and younger killed. Can you imagine the sorrow of the mothers and the cruelty of the soldiers as they tore the babies from their mothers arms!

Adolf Hitler, the Nazi dictator of Germany, was a ME person. He spread death as no person had ever done before. "Close your eyes to pity," he told his soldiers, "act brutally!" He was responsible for the slaughter of six million Jews.[1]

ME people are basically adult Joey's and Billy's, who are still fighting for the ball. There will be bad relationships as long as the interest is for ME to get the ball for myself. However, when the ball becomes *ours*, we can enjoy a beautiful game.

When children fight for the ball, we call it selfishness. It is an open expression of the self-will. That self-will does not evaporate with age. It is a basic *sin-root* problem.

God dealt with Jacob, and gave him a holy limp. He could then be reunited with his brother Esau. For the oil of good relationships to flow freely, the believer needs to experience both the "holy limp," and a "Gethsemane surrender." It was in Gethsemane that Jesus said, "Not my will, but thine be done." In the Gethsemane surrender, the believer gives up the ball, and turns his back on selfishness, jealousy, anger, and envy. The believer then goes from his Gethsemane surrender, and makes it a *way of life*, repenting and confessing along the way. This is what molds the character of a gracious, gentle, and kind person surrounded by friends as the hair turns gray and the years roll by.

Watch Out for Bitterness!

Selfishness is the vestibule, or the entry-way into the auditorium of bitterness. Selfish ME people seldom get what they think they really want. As a result, they are prime candidates for bitterness. Since they cannot get what they want from others, they turn bitter.

The Bible gives strong warnings against bitterness. "Get rid of all bitterness, rage and anger, brawling and slander, along with every form of malice" (Eph. 4:31;NIV). God is instructing us to put away all bitterness, to put off all malice. Malice is the desire to see something not so nice happen to another. It means rejoicing if some mischief befalls the person you do not care for.

Bitterness is, "a figurative term denoting that fretted and irritable state of mind that keeps a man in perpetual animosity — that inclines him to harsh and uncharitable opinions of men and things — that makes him sour, crabbed, and repulsive in his general demeanor — that brings a scowl over his face, and fuses venom into the words of his tongue."[2] The definition is pointed and painful! Who wants to become sour, crabbed, and repulsive?

Richard Halverson pointed to this problem in a devotional thought on growing old:

> You're going to meet an old man someday!
> Down the road ahead — ten, twenty, thirty years —

waiting there for you. He may be a seasoned, soft, gracious fellow, a gentleman who has grown old gracefully: surrounded by hosts of friends who call him blessed because of what his life has meant to them. He may be a bitter, disillusioned, dried up, cynical old buzzard without a good word for anybody; soured, friendless, and alone.

The kind of old man you will meet depends entirely on yourself, because that old man will be you.

His heart will be turning out what you've been putting in. Every little thought, every deed goes into this old man. He'll be exactly what you make him. Nothing more, nothing less. It's up to you. You'll have no one else to credit or blame.

The time to take care of that old man is right now, today, this week. Examine his motives, attitudes, goals. Check up on him. Work him over while he's still plastic, still in a formative condition. The day comes awfully soon when it's too late. The hardness sets in worse than paralysis. Character crystallizes, sets, gels. That's the finish.[3]

"I'm not a bitter person," you say. "There are only one or two people I have it in for." That is all it takes to completely ruin you, and destroy your character. Bitterness directed at one person is enough to make your very being crabbed and repulsive.

It seems very significant that the Bible instructs "Husbands, love your wives, and be not bitter against them" (Col. 3:19). Bitterness against one's partner is a common sin. The Bible strongly warns against this trap.

I read the sad story of John Mitchell's death in the November 10, 1988, issue of the *Washington Post*. I had a deep interest in the former United States attorney general, and his involvement in the Watergate scandal. He had been out of the public eye since he served time in a federal institution. He died on November 9, 1988, at age 75.

Once one of the most famous men in America, he was so reclusive in his final years that some neighbors said they never realized he had lived on their street. He walked to and from the office daily, rarely exchanging greetings with those he passed. He never smiled. He wouldn't acknowledge good morning. You'd say good morning, and he'd look away. He just walked up and down the street, puffing his pipe.

This man has been spiritually dead ever since he was indicted.

His wife, Martha, died alone of cancer in a New York hospital in 1976. It appears they were bitter against each other. It is sad to realize that friends and acquaintances of the Mitchell's have been hurt and wounded by their actions. These are some of the bitter harvests of being ME people. It is truly tragic that many others, including believers, are caught in this same trap of bitterness, and become crabbed, cynical old people.

Why did George Bush win the 1988 United States presidential election? In the spring of 1988, Mr. Bush was 16 percentage points behind his Democratic opponent. By November 8 Bush closed the gap, and easily won the election. How did he do it? In part, he understood that *WE* can win this election. He followed this principle, and won.

Those who followed the stories of 1988 know that on the winning team were names like Baker, Atwater, Teeter, Brady, and Fuller. Put all these names together, and add Bush, and they can say, WE won the 1988 election. George Bush was not too wrapped up in ME to take advice from WE. He won!

Dukakis followed the ME principle. In spite of being warned by memo and conference calls, nothing happened. Others said, Dukakis was making all the strategic decisions. He wanted to campaign on his own issues. The lesson is that, in Dukakis, you have a candidate who, when a match was lit in his vicinity, poured gasoline all over himself.[4]

That sounds like a ME person. And he lost!

ME people don't only lose elections, they lose friends, relationships, and the very fiber that makes life fulfilling.

Through the Choice Books ministry, WE can provide the eastern seaboard with Christian books on over 1,200 racks — we call them wire pulpits. ME could never do that!

The six most important words — I admit I made a mistake.
The five most important words — You did a good job.
The four most important words — What is your opinion?
The three most important words — If you please.
The two most important words — Thank you.
The one most important word — WE.

ME people — WE people! What do you really want to be? As Halverson pointed out, "The kind of old man . . . [let me say old person] . . . depends entirely on yourself . . . . It's up to you."[5] It is your choice!

Chapter 12

The Beauty of Accountability

The camera clicked, and the pictures it produced exposed the unaccounted life of a man considered by many as the nation's most powerful evangelist. A story in the *Washington Post* gave the nation a broadside view inside Jimmy Swaggart's private box, as he pursued a secret life.

"At times he wore hats, or sunglasses, or headbands, combing his blond hair down in front, as if he were hiding," says a woman who had been registered for some time at Tony's Motel.

Over the last two or three years, the motel owner says, he watched one of the country's most powerful Pentecostal holy men — a man who once called himself an "old fashioned, Holy Ghost-filled, shouting, weeping, soul-winning, gospel preaching preacher" — rent rooms here in the shadow of an ominous billboard with the words reading "Your Eternity is at stake."

The photographs of Swaggart's secret life "were dispatched to the Assemblies of God Board of Presbyters in Springfield, Missouri, and the latest Evangelical scandal broke."[1]

This tragedy is somewhat similar to one recorded in Joshua 7 about Achan, who secretly did his own thing — sinned — and as a result, Israel lost the battle at Ai.

Children sometimes have the idea that it is smart to know a secret they will not tell their friends. It runs like this, "I know something you don't. It is a secret; but I won't tell you what it is."

When I was a youngster, my brother made a wooden box with a padlock on it. His tightly locked box became a point of tension. He had something in the box he was hiding, and others wanted to know what it was.

Later, it became my box. I suppose I purchased it for a small fee. Like my brother, I kept the box locked. What did I have in it? Basically nothing that was for my good. It certainly did not contain things that promoted Christian maturity.

That box did not build good relationships with my family. If anything, it created tension and put distance in our relationships. I was locking up part of my life, and signaling to others that this part of me was none of their business.

Chalk up the box story to child's play if you want, *it is more than that.* Both the box story and the Swaggart tragedy reflect symptoms of the same root problem that destroys good relationships. Neither meet the biblical standard of ". . . as much as lieth in you, live peaceably with all men" (Rom. 12:18).

Hiding something from others, placing the worst side of us away in secrecy, and locking others out became part of our natural makeup as a result of sin. God created Adam and Eve to have fellowship with himself, and with each other. They began in a pure relationship with nothing between them and God. Henry Morris suggests that God may have had "a daily appointment time . . ." at which He met with them for ". . . communion and fellowship."[2]

Then they sinned! They were guilty! They had something to hide. The Bible says, "And they heard the voice of the Lord God walking in the garden in the cool of the day: and Adam and his wife hid themselves from the presence of the Lord God amongst the trees of the garden" (Gen. 3:8).

Morris comments, "On this occasion, however; instead of encountering Adam waiting expectantly for the daily time of fellowship, Adam was hiding among the trees, hoping to avoid seeing God altogether."[3]

Here is an *important principle* to keep in focus if you want to have a good relationship with others: Sin has implanted into the system of mankind the natural instinct to hide, to cover sin, and to keep secret boxes. It is the sinful instinct in man that says what I do is none of your business. It is that attitude, and the consequent actions, that quickly destroy relationships.

The editor of the *Mennonite Brethren Herald*, a Canadian magazine, let it be known that he was disturbed when another popular preacher suggested that "it is nobody else's business how he spends his money."

Editor Coggins wrote, "This man's 'own' money comes from royalties from the best-selling books he has sold in the Christian community. Is he really suggesting that those readers who have made him rich have no right to question what he has done with his money? Have we no right to demand accountability from our leaders? With the rampant individualism in modern society, is there no longer any such thing as mutual accountability in the Church?"[4]

People, because of their sinful nature, do not want to be accountable to each other. We want to have our secret boxes where no one else can come, and where we need not give an account to anyone. Non-accountability comes naturally, without effort, but it destroys relationships. Locked boxes of non-accountability destroy individual relationships, as well as sweeping across the spectrum of human relationships to destroy the world's most powerful evangelists. Between these two points are churches splitting and fragmenting, marriages deteriorating and breaking, families feuding, and friends parting ways.

Locked boxes literally lock people out, and chase them away. Locked boxes of non-accountability lock out close relationships. The more you hide, the more curious people become. As a result, you try to hide more and more. It becomes a vicious cycle.

Why Be Accountable?

1. Because it is biblical!

Refusing to be accountable for your life comes naturally — and hurts others. The Bible calls believers to a better way. It is called *Body life*. In the Church we are directly related to one another:

> We are to love one another.
> Build up one another.
> Give preference to one another in brotherly love.
> Be of the same mind toward one another.
> Admonish one another.
> Greet one another.
> Wait for one another.
> Care for one another.
> Serve one another.
> Bear one another's burdens.
> Confess one to another.
> Pray one for another.
> Forbear with one another.
> Comfort one another.
> Be kind one to another.
> Be at peace with one another.
> Forgive each other.
> And many more one anotherings in God's Word.

That does not sound like what I do is none of your business, rather, we are accountable to each other for our actions. First Corinthians 12:20-27 describes the body life of the believers. "But now are they many members, yet but one body. And the eye cannot say unto the hand, I have no need of thee: nor again the head to the feet, I have no need of you. Nay, much more those members of the body, which seem to be more feeble, are necessary: And those members of the body, which we think to be less honourable, upon these we bestow more abundant honour; and our uncomely parts have more abundant comeliness. For our comely parts have no need: but God hath tempered the body together, having given more abundant honour to that part which lacked: That there should be no schism in the body; but that the members should have the same care one for another. And whether one member suffer, all the members suffer with it; or one member be honoured, all the members rejoice with it. Now ye are the body of Christ, and members in particular" (1 Cor. 12:20-27).

There are many people in the Church, but only one Body. This biblical message is not the same as the one that our good old North American culture teaches. It tells you to go for the wealth, and make yourself successful. After all, you worked hard for it, it is all yours. It is nobody's business what you do with it. The gospel, according to the present wealthy world, would be paraphrased like this; "The eye must say to the hand, what I do does not concern you: or the hand to the feet, go and mind you own business. I seem to be stronger than you, you really aren't necessary in my life."

Only in the context of accountability can we have the same care for one another, or help one who lacks, or suffer with one another, or celebrate joys with each other.

Only in the context of accountability can there be a close relationship. This is true in all relationships: marriage, family, friend with friend, church, work, and social interactions. One of the main ingredients of being at peace with each other is accountability.

2. *Because it builds trust.*

It is easier to trust people who are accountable. Anytime you hide something from another, you break down trust. When trust is broken down, the relationship moves from closeness to distance. We trust giving a dollar to a person who is accountable. If we are suspicious that he may use it to buy cigarettes, we will not spare him a dime. We give with less hesitation to an organization with open books than one that expects blind trust because they are "in the Lord's work."

Just as we give to the accountable people, and withhold from the non-accountable, we also give our friendships to the accountable, and tend to withhold it from the non-accountable.

We had Watergate, later Irangate, and then in the religious world, we had what someone called Pearlygate. All of these scandals involved secret boxes, and non-accountability. Our nation becomes enraged when they think the president may be trying to hide something. His credibility instantly drops. The Pearlygate scandals brought a reproach on the Church, and the name of Christ. The boxes of hush money that was to be used in the Lord's work apparently was used to hide sin. That act alone shattered trust.

The common teenage myth, "It is nobody's business what I do!" is sin. It destroys trust between parents and teenagers. The teenage son who has no boxes to hide and is accountable is trusted by his father. They have very few words about using the car. There is no argument of where he is going, and what time he will come home. Accountability has already established trust.

Parents often program unaccountability into their children by their lifestyle, then expect accountability to come out. *That is absurd.* What you plant by example into the lives of your small children is what will grow when they become older.

The apostle Paul was concerned that his life, and the life of the church leaders, be an expression of honesty and accountability.

"But thanks be to God, which put the same earnest care into the heart of Titus for you. For indeed he accepted the exhortation; but being more forward, of his own accord he went unto you. And we have sent with him the brother, whose praise is in the gospel throughout all the churches; And not that only, but who was also chosen of the churches to travel with us with this grace, which is administered by us to the glory of the same Lord, and declaration of your ready mind: Avoiding this, that no man should blame us in this abundance which is administered by us: Providing for honest things, not only in the sight of the Lord, but also in the sight of men" (2 Cor. 8:16-21).

Paul was concerned about accountability to God and man. "Providing for honest things, not only in the sight of the Lord, but also in the sight of men."

Anytime you try to hide anything from anyone, whether you are the president of the United States, or one person relating to another, trust is broken down. Accountability builds trust.

3. *It builds successful lives.*

Jesus had 12 people working with Him during His short

earthly ministry. Judas was a selfish person who was not fully accountable for his actions or intentions. He came to the Lord's Supper with his boxes along. He was hiding something from the rest of his colleagues. He left that night without informing any of them where he was going, and what he was going to do. He became history's most infamous betrayer. He paid a high price for being unaccountable.

On the other hand, Peter denied the Lord Jesus three times. Later, Jesus called him to account, and asked him three times, "Do you love me?" Peter assured the Lord that he did love Him. Peter became one of the Early Church's most notable workers, and wrote part of the New Testament. He was *accountable,* and he was *successful.*

Ted Engstrom has written more than 30 books that have helped thousands of Christians make the best use of their time and talent. He has been president of Youth for Christ International, and president of World Vision. I have personally received much help and encouragement from his writings on management and leadership. His ministry has been successful in blessing many people.

What kind of man is Engstrom? Is he a man who sends signals for others to go mind their own business? No, he is not. Notice what he says about accountability, "Everyone needs to be accountable, not only to God, but to another human being."[5]

More than 10 years ago Engstrom wrote, "For about eight years I have been meeting five other men for breakfast in a restaurant. It is not a prayer meeting, but we pray together. It is not a Bible study, but we refer to the Word of God together. We share with each other. There is nothing we would not do for each other . . . . We are accountable to each other, for we uphold each other in many ways. I am accountable to them; they are accountable to me. A leader needs to be part of a peer group."[6]

In the *Christian Leadership Letter,* edited by Engstrom and Dayton, they wrote, "At the one-to-one, person-to-person level we should seek to be accountable to someone for as many areas of our lives as possible (and to permit others to ask us to hold them accountable).

"Holding others accountable, and being held accountable is

at the root of the life that is Christian. Our Lord is going to hold us accountable for all the gifts He has given us. 'By this all men will know that you are My disciples, if you have love one for another' (John 13:35;NAS). That kind of love demands accountability. But the rewards are great, not only in satisfaction of accomplishment, but in our relationship with another as well."[7]

Do you understand why Engstrom is a successful man?

James Dobson has experienced a remarkable success with the Focus on the Family ministry. Following the Bakker, Roberts, and Swaggart episode, Dobson wrote in the April 1987 *Focus on the Family Newsletter,* "We must not leave the reputation of the Kingdom in the hands of anyone who lacks strict accountability to associates who can help keep him on the path." Focus on the Family belongs to the Evangelical Council for Financial Accountability. Dobson further comments, "Several times per year, these men and women who serve on our board ask me to account for every dollar contributed to Focus on the Family."

Dobson then makes this point, "Everyone needs to report to someone." Your success rate in being a friend, in ministering to others, and having close relationships is very closely tied to the extent of your accountability.

4. It builds closeness.

"Behold, how good and how pleasant it is for brethren to dwell together in unity!" (Ps. 133:1).

Accountability brings about a pleasant unity, a feeling of closeness and an assurance of acceptance.

What happens in family relationships when parents have *programmed* accountability into the lifestyles of their children? It works like this. Dad comes into the house to pick up his wallet, and tells his wife that he is going to the hardware store to buy some grass seed. "I should be back soon," he adds as he leaves. Or the son says, "I am going to K-Mart to pick up a notebook." That kind of simple respect cultivates closeness and establishes accountability at the very grassroots. When it is programmed into our system, it will be easy to be accountable to others. It will be easier for those children to be accountable to authority whenever they meet it. They will get along with their teachers, their friends, and their boss. And later, their relationships with their spouse and family will be much stronger.

Parents who give their children the impression that it is no one else's business what they do are programming devastation into the lives of their children.

How does accountability affect the work place? It makes a big difference in the working atmosphere. A dangerous threat in the work place is when the boss is away, and no one else knows where he is. This encourages suspicion, leaves the employees guessing, puts distance between them, and makes them feel unimportant. It is not good for the boss himself. He becomes vulnerable to many social temptations.

It is said that there are four types of employees:

> — the one who acts, and reports back (this is
>   accountability);
> — the one who asks what to do;
> — the one who wants to be told what to do;
> — the one who has to be found.

It is clear which one does his job best and will relate well with the manager. The person who says at the end of the day, "If it is okay, I'll be leaving now. I am going to see my folks over the weekend, and plan to see you Monday morning," will be closer to the employer than the one who punches the clock, gives that "don't ask me anything" look, and slams the door.

Richard Strauss wrote, "Psychologists tell us that we only understand as much of ourselves as we share with others, and I have found that to be true in my own life. The more of my inner life I share with my wife, the more I begin to understand myself. It we are not transparent with others — have never verbalized our hopes and fears, values and priorities, dreams and aspirations, failures and discouragements, joys and sorrows, needs and wants, feelings and frustrations — we probably do not fully understand ourselves, and therefore are not growing."[8]

Accountability builds closeness. Solomon wrote, "Two are better than one, because they have a good return for their work: If one falls down, his friend can help him up. But pity the man who falls and has no one to help him up!" (Eccles. 4:9-10;NIV).

5. It builds godliness.

"As iron sharpens iron, so one man sharpens another" (Prov. 27:17;NIV).

Man was made, not for solitude, but for companionship. It is only as a social being that his powers and affections are expanded. Iron sharpens iron. Steel whetted against a knife, sharpens the edge. So the collision of different minds whets each the edge of the other.

In the sympathies of friendship, when a mind is dull and the countenance overcast, a word from a friend puts an edge upon the blunted energy and exhilarates the countenance.[9]

"Nothing happens if people do not hold themselves accountable. And yet Christian organizations in general, and local churches in particular, often are at their weakest when it comes to holding themselves accountable. One noted secular psychologist sums it up by observing that the Early Church discovered the tremendous social value of confessing our sins to one another — being accountable. But the Roman Church came along and said that we only had to confess our sins to the priest. When the Protestants came on the scene, they made it worse! They said we only had to confess our sins to God. Then Freud blew the whole thing; he said we didn't have any sins to confess."[10]

But we do have sins to confess! The Bible teaches we are to confess our faults one to another. This needs to be practiced in order to have good relationships and to live victoriously for Christ. Confession is very effective when practiced one to one. Confession of wrongdoing to your fellow believer helps you overcome your evil habits.

Certain sins may require regular accountability in order to be victorious. It may mean you need to ask someone to check on you on a regular basis.

J. Carl Laney wrote, "Personal accountability to a pastor friend has proven effective in my own life to help me avoid certain sins and temptations."[11]

My mind goes to young people who are struggling with sin, and are not enjoying their Christian walk. They are not loyal to their commitment to the Church. They give their parents heavy hearts. They refuse to be held *accountable*. They do not want to give an account of where they go, when, and why.

I think of other youth whose lives are a true testimony for Christ. They are a joy to their parents, and an exciting part of the Church. They relate well with others. They are the accountable ones.

The line is clear — accountability fosters godliness, excellence, and mature character. Unaccountability encourages faulty character, irresponsibility, and heaps hurts and pains on others they come in contact with.

If only Swaggart would have realized the beauty of accountability, his preaching might still be heard in many parts of the world. If he would have developed the habit of telling his associates where he went and what he was doing, he may not have fallen prey to the devil's trap. The camera would not have clicked, and caught him in the wrong place.

Accountability! Is it too much bother? Remember this principle: The things that build good relationships take work! The things that destroy our friendships come naturally.

Accountability is not that difficult. It is just a matter of programming it into your lifestyle. When it is there it becomes a part of you, and becomes as easy as walking.

When you start sending out "it's none of your business" signals, you can pick up your pen and begin writing your relationship obituary — unless the other person is willing to suffer on your behalf.

When accountability becomes a part of your lifestyle, it makes life so much smoother for people around you. You make them feel needed, and their appreciation for you grows!

Accountability is a matter of choice. If you refuse to be held accountable, here are some of the results.

1. You will not have close, lasting and supportive friends.

2. You definitely are not a leader, manager, or teaching role model.

3. People will not enjoy working for you or with you.

4. Inner joy, satisfaction, and contentment will always elude you.

5. You will be very vulnerable to sin, like Achan was, whose sin brought defeat to Israel, and resulted in his own death.

6. You can expect to die alone and bitter as people allow you to "mind your own business." (But do not forget, you *must* still give an account to God.)

Jesus Christ left a better example. Mark, writing about Jesus, wrote, "And he ordained twelve, that they should be with him . . ." (Mark 3:14). He called 12 to be with Him, and He was accountable to them.

Yes, Jesus drew the crowds, ministered to them, healed their diseases, and enlightened hungry minds. He was committed to die for the sins of the whole world, and yet, He gave priority to His disciples. Jesus said, "Henceforth I call you not servants . . . but I have called you friends; for all things I have heard of my Father I have made known unto you" (John 15:15).

Jesus Christ opened himself to His disciples. He gave up everything. But yet, His kingdom still stands, and He will reign forever!

Accountability makes you more effective in His kingdom.

Chapter 13

Harmony in the Workplace

There were many oak trees growing in the woods on my father's farm that made good building material. When he needed lumber to build or repair a building, he would fell a tree, cut it into logs, and take them to the sawmill.

There was a little catch to the cutting part. My father did not have a chain saw at that time, so whenever he needed more lumber he would hitch the horses to the wagon, take the crosscut saw, tell me to come along, and head for the woods. After we had felled the tree, the two of us would agree (by his command) to cut the tree into shorter lengths.

The two of us worked together, cutting logs with a crosscut saw. How well we performed depended on how well we worked together. If I followed Dad's instructions, and blended well with his motions, we got along fine. We cut logs! There was harmony as we learned to work together.

Whenever two people plan to cut logs with a crosscut saw, it is a must for them to work together. If they work together harmoniously, the job can soon be done. If they work against each other, it is almost impossible to get the job done. Good cutting relationships are a *must!*

So it is with our work. Good relationships are a must on the job. Work is a part of you. "In your lifetime, you will spend about 40 percent of your waking hours on your job."[1]

One of the important places to practice godly relationships is on the job. Your job can be a place of enjoyment, or a place of dread. It depends largely on your relationship with the people you work with, and those you work for.

Proper attitudes are a priority with God. Improper and unscriptural attitudes have done much damage in the marketplace. Anger and bitterness between labor and management has crippled entire cities with strife and strikes.

Improper attitudes bring feelings of resentment between the employee and employer. Employees walk off the job in order to show the boss a thing or two. Managers fire employees without any show of mercy.

A Fairfax County man was gunned down and murdered by a man who apparently "harbored a grudge that festered over the years."[2] It was suspected that the man who lashed out in bitter murder blamed the victim for dismissing him from a job where they had both worked 12 years earlier.

Bitterness, strife, envy, jealousy, selfishness, and related sins of the heart have no mercy on anyone. These sins will drive both employee and employer to take further ungodly action against each other, even to the point of murder.

The spread between the seed of bitterness and murder is cluttered with devilish actions too numerous to be listed. A few are such sins as hatred and strife, expressed by the cold shoulder and sour tongue, and lording it over each other.

Does God address the subject of relationships in the work place? Yes, He does! He gave us some clear guidelines in the Scriptures. God has certain goals He wants to accomplish through the believer on the job. God has given us principles to follow in helping us accomplish His goals in the marketplace where we work.

First, let's look at what the worker's basic foundational attitude should be toward work. If we master the teachings of Ephesians 4:28, and submit to it, we have come a long way toward harmony and unity in the work place. "Let him that stole steal no more: but rather let him labour, working with his hands the thing which is good, that he may have to give to him that needeth."

There are three principles in this passage.

1. Stop stealing!

You may say to yourself, "I am not a thief." But, do you fudge on your time card, taking a little extra here and there? Do you use the boss's truck to run little errands for yourself? Do you figure you are underpaid, so there is nothing wrong with taking one 2 x 4 every night until you have enough material to build a shed? These things are stealing. *Stop stealing.*

2. Do something good!

The believer is to be in a work that is honest, good, and beneficial to others. We are to be involved in a work that contributes to the well-being of the community. Businesses and employment that are questionable in the light of biblical standards should be avoided.

This reminds me of a certain lady who worked at an airport newsstand. She had to take the money from people who bought adult magazines. She was not totally at ease about it, and indicated that she did not like to do it, but hoped God would forgive her.

Our work should be the kind that has God's blessing upon it, and does not need God's forgiveness.

3. Work to give! Live to give!

". . . That he may have to give to him that needeth." Whoever heard of that? Don't we get jobs so that we can buy a new car? Or go to the Holy Land? Or buy property? Or acquire a resort? I am not ruling out any of these as wrong. Don't you think, though, that often our primary reason for earning money is to acquire something for ourselves?

As a young lad, I had wanted a wagon. My father was in a difficult financial situation at the time, and could not afford those expensive toys for his children. So, I went to work washing windows and doing other chores for my Aunt Emma. Finally, when I had almost earned $17.02 for the wagon, my oldest brother chipped in and gave a few coins toward my goal. There were many good aspects about this experience. I learned what it was to work for 50 cents a day, and save toward a goal. I had to please my employers, Aunt Emma and Uncle Red. But completely missing was the principle of earning something in order to be able to *give*. I believe that my spiritual growth over the years has brought me to the realization of the importance of this principle.

When the worker labors under the principle of working to be able to help others, it sets the whole atmosphere of the job. This worker will be easy to get along with, easy to be trusted, and a joy to work with.

We think of giving as something we do for poor people on the other side of the world. If you have really caught the meaning of this principle, it will have its effect on the people who are close enough to see the sweat roll down your face. It starts right where you live and work.

I was employed by George Copp for many years. He would occasionally come by with a box of donuts or milk shakes for his employees. That was a good investment. It set a positive attitude in the air. It showed an attitude of giving and sharing. The person who is not too tight to pass out coke or tea occasionally is exercising the privilege of giving. I can assure you that such a person is appreciated more on the job than the one who will not spare a dime.

Live to give; work to be able to give.

The second foundational attitude toward work is to work to provide your basic needs.

"Now about brotherly love we do not need to write to you, for you yourselves have been taught by God to love each other. And in fact, you do love all the brothers throughout Macedonia. Yet we urge you, brothers, to do so more and more. Make it your ambition to lead a quiet life, to mind your own business and to work with your hands, just as we told you, so that your daily life may win the respect of outsiders and so that you will not be dependent on anybody" (1 Thess. 4:9-12;NIV).

Here are some guidelines from this passage.

1. Love one another. Whether you are an employee or an employer, the rule is love one another.

2. Aim to live quietly and peacefully with others. Learn how to work together to get the job done and be able to go home in peace at night. Discern the leader's goals, then "grab your end of the saw" and do your job well.

3. Work with your hands so your daily life will win the respect of others.

4. Provide for your own needs so that you will not need to sponge off others.

"Neither did we eat any man's bread for nought; but wrought with labour and travail night and day, that we might not be chargeable to any of you: Not because we have not power, but to make ourselves an ensample unto you to follow us. For even when we were with you, this we commanded you, that if any would not work, neither should he eat. For we hear that there are some which walk among you disorderly, working not at all, but are busybodies. Now them that are such we command and exhort by our Lord Jesus Christ, that with quietness they work, and eat their own bread" (2 Thess. 3:8-12).

1. Do not be idle, wasting your time.

2. Work so you can provide the daily needs of yourself and your household.

3. Work in an orderly disciplined manner, it is good for everyone around you.

A believer also needs the foundational principle of not coveting. "And now, brethren, I commend you to God, and to the word of his grace, which is able to build you up, and to give you an inheritance among all them which are sanctified. I have coveted no man's silver, gold, or apparel. Yea, ye yourselves know, that these hands have ministered unto my necessities, and to them that were with me. I have shewed you all things, how that so labouring ye ought to support the weak, and to remember the words of the Lord Jesus, how he said, It is more blessed to give than to receive" (Acts 20:32-35).

Paul, in speaking to the Christians, told them that he had not coveted their silver, gold, or clothing. He said he had worked to supply his own needs, and the needs of those with him. His hands had shown care for the needs of his careworkers. He had demonstrated how they ought to support the weak, and reminded them that it is more blessed to give than to receive.

These principles are like foundations for buildings — solid and firm. Once they have become a part of you, building on them will make a definite difference for you on the job.

These attitudes are in sharp contrast to the young rebel that walks into a place of business with his hair looking like there is no barber within 90 miles, his shirttail out over torn jeans, and shoe strings dangling, and asks, "Got any job for me?" in a tone that suggests, "Hey, man, you owe me a good living."

Let's move on to the workplace, and examine from the Bible what God's standards are for getting along with each other on the job.

We will look at five different passages of Scripture. Each passage refers to slaves or servants. Instruction is given to both the servants and masters. The equation in today's world would be the employee and employer. However, bear in mind, the standards are the same today as they were for servants and masters when the New Testament was written.

Let's look at the "Handbook of Employee-Employer Relationships," and see what the rules are.

1. Obey as you would Christ.

"Servants, be obedient to them that are your masters according to the flesh, with fear and trembling, in singleness of your heart, as unto Christ; Not with eyeservice, as menpleasers; but as the servants of Christ, doing the will of God from the heart; With good will doing service, as to the Lord, and not to men: Knowing that whatsoever good thing any man doeth, the same shall he receive of the Lord, whether he be bond or free. And, ye masters, do the same things unto them, forbearing threatening: knowing that your Master also is in heaven; neither is there respect of persons with him" (Eph. 6:5-9).

The number one rule on the job is obedience and submission to the boss. You are to obey him as you would obey Jesus Christ. You are to respect your employer and have a concern to please him with a sincere heart. In Titus we are told to obey in all things (Titus 2:9).

You may be thinking, "But you don't know my boss, you don't know how unreasonable he is, and how demanding he can become." That is not the issue. It really does not matter whether you think the boss deserves it or not; you are to obey him in all things.

There is only one exception. If he asks you to do something

that is in conflict with God's Word, remember that obedience to God and His Word must precede any other authority. The Bible says, ". . . We ought to obey God rather than men" (Acts 5:29).

If your employer asks something contrary to God's Word, you must kindly appeal, and explain that you cannot violate God's Word and your conscience. In all other areas, you are endeavoring to obey him as you would Christ.

2. Work as if you were employed by Christ himself.

"Servants, obey in all things your masters according to the flesh; not with eyeservice, as menpleasers; but in singleness of heart, fearing God: And whatsoever ye do, do it heartily, as to the Lord, and not unto men; Knowing that of the Lord ye shall receive the reward of the inheritance: for ye serve the Lord Christ. But he that doeth wrong shall receive for the wrong which he hath done: and there is no respect of persons" (Col. 3:22-25).

Again, here is the admonition to obey your employer. You are to work for him with sincerity, and with all your heart; not only when the boss is there, or others are watching, but as though Jesus Christ was there in person and you were doing the work for Him. Work as if Jesus Christ were your employer.

According to the Bible, it is in fact Christ you are serving. ". . . It is the Lord Christ you are serving" (Col. 3:24;NIV).

It is Christ who is ultimately going to reward you for your work. The person who does wrong will receive the consequences for his wrongdoing. There is no respect to the person's position, whether employee or employer. The way you serve your employer is the way you serve Christ. Martin Luther said, "A dairymaid can milk cows to the glory of God."[3]

During my days of working as a carpenter, there were some jobs we had to do that were not very pleasant. It helped make the job more pleasant to realize that I was really working for Christ as we put up 2 x 4's. It certainly would have been helpful to me had I realized this when I was a teenage son helping my father carry manure out of the cattle barn on a cold winter day. Whether you are milking cows, building houses, cleaning out calf barns, punching a computer, or driving a delivery truck, do it as unto the Lord himself. Ultimately, Christ is your employer. It is not only your employer you are serving, but Christ.

3. Adorn the doctrine of God.

"Exhort servants to be obedient unto their own masters, and to please them well in all things; not answering again; Not purloining, but shewing all good fidelity; that they may adorn the doctrine of God our Saviour in all things" (Titus 2:9-10).

A major goal of your job is to "adorn the doctrine of God our Saviour in all things." This means you are to do your work in a way that will make the teachings of Jesus Christ attractive and appealing to your earthly employer. You are to do your work in a way that is pleasing to your employer; you are not to argue or talk back; you are forbidden to take a little of this or that — no pilfering of any kind. Why? So that your work will draw others to the gospel of Jesus Christ.

If you are paid for working eight hours a day, and walk out early without authority or understanding; you are stealing time. That brings disgrace to the gospel of Jesus Christ. Your good conduct, your dedication to excellent work, and your righteous life will adorn the teachings of Christ, and draw your employer to Christ. Employee, that is your mission.

Oswald Chambers wrote, "The stars do their work without fuss; God does His work without fuss; and saints do their work without fuss."[4]

4. Give reverence to God's name.

You are to honor and respect your employer. You are to consider him worthy of the fullest respect. He is the one who provides you with work and a paycheck. There is still a greater reason why you should give honor and respect to your employer. The Bible gives the command to honor and the reason why.

"Let as many servants as are under the yoke count their own masters worthy of all honour, that the name of God and his doctrine be not blasphemed" (1 Tim. 6:1).

One way of honoring your employer is by trying to make him or her successful. The harder you work at making the boss successful, the *more successful you will be.* The more you fuss and manipulate to bring the boss down, the more you lower yourself.

Another way of honoring the employer is to give *quality* and *quantity* work. It has been said that too many people quit looking for work once they have a job.

Shoddy work and short cuts bring slander against the name of God. Unbelievers will say if that is what a Christian is like, they don't want any part of it. You do not need to choose if you will witness for the name of God; rather, your attitude toward your employer, your work, and you yourself are a witness.

Suppose your employer is a believer. Can you then take things for granted and relax your standards? Absolutely not! You are to give them even more respect "because they are brethren." Christian organizations ought to employ the highest of biblical standards and respect for one another. It is a double shame when Christian organizations slander God's name through bickering and disrespectful conduct.

5. Find favor with God.

You will be favored by God if you are submissive to your masters with all respect, even if they are harsh and unreasonable.

"Servants, be subject to your masters with all fear; not only to the good and gentle, but also to the froward. For this is thankworthy, if a man for conscience toward God endure grief, suffering wrongfully. For what glory is it, if, when ye be buffeted for your faults, ye shall take it patiently? but if, when ye do well, and suffer for it, ye take it patiently, this is acceptable with God. For even hereunto were ye called: because Christ also suffered for us, leaving us an example, that ye should follow his steps: Who did no sin, neither was guile found in his mouth: Who, when he was reviled, reviled not again; when he suffered, he threatened not; but committed himself to him that judgeth righteously: Who his own self bare our sins in his own body on the tree, that we, being dead to sins, should live unto righteousness: by whose stripes ye were healed. For ye were as sheep going astray; but are now returned unto the Shepherd and Bishop of your souls" (1 Pet. 2:18-25).

Moaning and groaning, complaining and fussing, gossiping and tattling about the boss is not in God's will. When we continue faithfully and respectfully, even when our superiors may not be what they ought to be, we find favor with God.

We often think the grass is greener on the other side of the fence. We often feel it must be better somewhere else. God may have placed you in your job for a reason. He may want you to learn to live in these circumstances. King Solomon spent his lifetime trying to find the right circumstances that would bring him satisfaction. Escaping from your circumstances may simply mean shuffling the problem from one job to another. There are times when God wants you to suffer for His sake. This finds favor with Him.

The account of Joseph in the Bible is a touching story of a man who suffered for doing good. He refused to give in to the sexual temptation from Potiphar's wife. She then made a false accusation against Joseph, which lead to dismissal from his job, and being thrown into prison. He did not become bitter against God while he suffered for doing right. He found favor with God. (See Gen. 39.)

If you are having conflicts with your boss, God may be trying to teach you something about biblical submission to authority.[5]

What about the employer — doesn't the Bible speak to him? Yes, it does! "And, ye masters, do the same things unto them, forbearing threatening: knowing that your Master also is in heaven; neither is there respect of persons with him" (Eph. 6:9).

Masters, employers, you are to use the same principles toward your employees. "And masters, treat your slaves the same way" (NIV). ". . . Act on the same [principle] toward them" (AMP).

Give them respect, treat them with dignity, love them wholeheartedly as if they were Jesus Christ himself. The way you treat your employees is really the way you treat Jesus Christ.

The Bible strictly forbids threatening your employees. ". . . Give up threatening" (NAS). "Do not threaten them" (NIV). ". . . Give up threatening and using violent and abusive words" (AMP).

You are not to rattle a threat of firing over their head to get more work out of them. If they need to be relieved from their job, you must act in a responsible way, fully explaining why they must be dismissed, and tell them what to do to make corrections in their life.

Employer, you are responsible to God who is in heaven.

God is the master of both the employer and the employee, and please notice, God does not show favoritism or respect because you are the boss. You, the employer, are accountable to God.

The task of the employee to the employer is to give quality work. The responsibility of the employer to the employee is to give quality of life. A godly employer will see to it that his employees are able to provide for themselves and their family; just as Paul did in Acts: ". . . these hands have ministered unto my necessities, and to them that were with me" (Acts 20:34).

"Masters, give unto your servants that which is just and equal; knowing that ye also have a Master in heaven" (Col. 4:1).

The manager needs to communicate with the employees, delegate, and permit them to do the job. He needs to feel their hurts, and accept them as persons.

If employers and employees will follow the biblical principles in the workplace, they will experience peace, joy, and unity that will be deeply satisfying, and draw others to Jesus Christ.

Chapter 14

Authority and Our Relationships with Others

George was a man who had not had a close relationship with anyone for a long period of time. His relationship with his wife was only bearable. He was not close to his children, nor did he have a strong tie with a local church. Eventually, there were few friends or relatives who maintained an ongoing relationship with him. He slowly but surely offended his neighbors, and became alienated from his family. He died with no blue ribbons in good relationships, and very few people attended his funeral. There was another noteworthy characteristic about George; he *did not* have a healthy and biblical respect for authority.

Is there a connection with an individual's attitude toward authority and his ability to get along well with others? Does it affect his relationship with his spouse? The answer is *YES!*

Disrespect for authority, ranging from disobedience to parents, to school, to church leadership, and to the authority of national government, will eventually translate into inability to develop and maintain good relationships with others.

The young person who fails in cultivating a proper relationship with authority on the family level will have problems in the school, in the church, and with the laws of the land. Eventually, it will affect his relationship with the King of kings, the Lord Jesus Christ.

I think of many people about my age whose marriages have gone through severe stress, separation, and even divorce. One of the glaring faults of many of these friends is their attitude toward authority, their determination to take their own way, and especially noteworthy is their relationship and attitude toward their father.

The bottom line is simply this. You cannot have a bitter, rebellious, jealous, and stubborn attitude toward people in leadership and authority, and still develop and maintain good relationships with others. A wrong attitude toward authority on any level affects all other relationships.

Why? Because your attitude toward authority eventually translates into a lifestyle.

If you are one of those "he-men," and take things into your own hands and do what you want to, regardless of the church's position, do not be surprised if your wife will eventually catch on and do the same to you. This will devastate your marriage relationship. Your son will catch on, too. He will think, "I know Mom and Dad do not like it, but there is something in me that draws me to it. I will do it anyway." These attitudes shatter family relationships.

An unhealthy, unbiblical attitude toward authority develops into an unscriptural lifestyle that makes you difficult to get along with. A spirit that is not in subjection to authority will find it difficult to be in subjection to the opinions of friends and family.

What does the Bible say about believers' attitudes toward authority?

"Let every soul be subject unto the higher powers. For there is no power but of God: the powers that be are ordained of God. Whosoever therefore resisteth the power, resisteth the ordinance of God: and they that resist shall receive to themselves damnation. For rulers are not a terror to good works, but to the evil. Wilt thou then not be afraid of the power? do that which is good, and thou shalt have praise of the same: For he is the minister of God to thee for good. But if thou do that which is evil, be afraid; for he beareth not the sword in vain: for he is the minister of God, a revenger to execute wrath upon him that doeth evil. Wherefore ye must needs be subject, not only for wrath, but also for conscience sake. For this cause pay ye tribute also: for they are God's ministers, attending continually upon this very thing" (Rom. 13:1-6).

1. God is the One who established authority.

2. Rebelling against authority is rebelling against God.

3. Those who resist or set themselves up against authority bring down judgment on themselves.

4. The person in authority is God's servant for good.

5. Be in submission, as a matter of principle, and for conscience' sake.

6. They are to give their time attending to governing duties.

7. Pay your taxes, respect authority, and honor them for the position they hold.

Our theme is good relationships. What does our attitude toward authority have to do with getting along with each other? Notice verse 2, ". . . they that resist shall receive to themselves damnation . . . they who have opposed will receive condemnation upon themselves" (NAS).

Every husband, and every father and mother are authorities under God's order. Husbands, when you married your wife, you became chief director of the home. Wives, you joined your husband, and became vice president of the home. When your first child was born, you became authorities with the responsibility to teach that child about God.

Parents, when your child was conceived in the mother's womb, he inherited a sinful and rebellious nature. When your child was born, he was ready to scream for his own way. He was born with disrespect for authority. You are now the authority God put over that child. You have the responsibility to teach that child to subject himself to God's authority. If you, as the parents, are not subject to higher authority, your own example will come back to haunt you. Your own children will most likely respect authority the way you taught them by your example. As disrespect is passed from you to the next generation, it eventually returns directly back to you. Therefore, your relationship with your offspring is affected.

There is a connection with your attitude toward authority, and your ability to be close to your partner, your family, and those around you. ". . . those who oppose will receive condemnation upon themselves." Tell me, what is more condemning than a failure in relationships?

What else does the Bible say?

"Remember those who lead you, who spoke the word of God to you; and considering the result of their conduct, imitate their faith" (Heb. 13:7;NAS).

"Remember your leaders, who spoke the word of God to you. Consider the outcome of their way of life and imitate their faith" (NIV).

Here are some thoughts from the Amplified New Testament. "Observe attentively" "Consider their manner of living" "Imitate their *faith.* " (It does not say failures, but faith.)

"Obey them that have the rule over you, and submit yourselves: for they watch for your souls, as they that must give account, that they may do it with joy, and not with grief: for that is unprofitable for you" (Heb. 13:17).

". . . Let them do this with joy, and not with grief, for this would be *unprofitable for you* " (NAS).

Disrespect, rebellion, and disobedience to authority are *unprofitable* to you. It translates into bad relationships any way you think about it.

David and Jonathan are two people in Old Testament history who are known for their close relationship. Jonathan's friendship began with David on the day of David's return from the victory over the champion of Gath. That friendship continued until the day of Jonathan's death.

Jonathan's father, King Saul, became very jealous over David. In his wrath and anger, he attempted to kill David. The Bible says, ". . . Saul sought him everyday, but God delivered him not into his hand" (1 Sam. 23:14). David fled to the wilderness to escape Saul's jealous rage. "And Jonathan Saul's son arose and went to David into the wood, and strengthened his hand in God" (1 Sam. 23:16).

In their relationship, they made a covenant before the Lord. "Then Jonathan and David made a covenant, because he loved him as his own soul" (1 Sam. 18:3). "And Jonathan said to David, Go in peace, forasmuch as we have sworn both of us in the name of the Lord, saying, The Lord be between me and thee, and between my seed and thy seed for ever. And he arose and departed: and Jonathan went into the city" (1 Sam. 20:42).

When David heard of Jonathan's death, he wrote this response, "I grieve for you, Jonathan my brother; you were very dear to me, Your love for me was very wonderful, more wonderful than that of women" (2 Sam. 1:26;NIV).

This indeed was an outstanding friendship. Is there anything significant about the attitudes in their relationship? Jonathan was Saul's oldest son. During his father's lifetime, he was regarded as the heir to the throne. From the people's perspective, Jonathan should be king. But God chose David for the throne.

Here is a prime setting for a fight for the top slot. *All* the rules of human nature say they should be enemies rather than best of friends. However, they are the ultimate example in the Scripture of maintaining good relationships.

Why were they good friends? What was there secret or formula? It is in their attitude toward authority! First, notice Jonathan's attitude toward David.

"And he said unto him, Fear not: for the hand of Saul my father shall not find thee; and thou shalt be king over Israel, and I shall be next unto thee; and that also Saul my father knoweth" (1 Sam. 23:17).

"You will be king! I will be second to you!" Imagine this miracle attitude! Jonathan, the oldest son of Saul says to David, "You will assume the throne I have a right to by birth. It is God's order."

There was no jockeying for the top slot, to be in control, or to lord it over the other. That would have killed the relationship. Jonathan had a submissive attitude in recognizing God's call upon David as king. As a result, their relationship could prosper.

It is equally important to notice David's response toward Jonathan and Saul even after he realized that God had called him to be king over the nation of Israel. He continued to cultivate a good relationship with Jonathan. He never rebelled against King Saul, or challenged his position of authority. David never attempted to take control before God called him to the throne.

Recognizing that our attitude toward authority does affect our relationship with others, where do we go from here?

1. Cultivate scriptural attitudes toward authority.

Practice seeing it from God's perspective. Become familiar with what the Scripture says about authority. Make its teaching a way of life. Mold it into your life so firmly that you will be able to spot a counterfeit attitude before it grabs hold of your thoughts and actions. Beware lest the cartoonist in your newspaper influence your attitudes toward authority in a wrong way.

I have lived during the terms of both popular and unpopular presidents. Lyndon B. Johnson won the 1964 election by a landslide. During his administration, the Vietnam War reached its height. As many people began to doubt statements made by officials in his administration, we were introduced to a credibility gap. His popularity dropped. The slogan for some became, "Out of the way with L.B.J."

Was that a scriptural attitude for believers? I say *NO*. We must be acquainted with the Scriptures so we do not become caught up with the popular slogans that do not honor God. Develop biblical attitudes toward all authority, from your parents all the way to the king of the land.

2. Work to make your leader successful.

In reference to church leaders, the Bible says, ". . . Obey them so that their work will be a joy . . ." (Heb. 13:17;NIV). It is your responsibility to pray for your leaders, and help them be successful. When you pray for their success, you will find yourself having better attitudes toward them. Those whose aim is to make their pastors, leaders, and superiors successful also tend to get along well with them. Their relationship is a success. Those who make it a point to humiliate, work against, undercut, or belittle their leaders are destroying relationships for themselves and those around them.

There are those who are jealous because another is called to leadership. They will not be working to make the leader successful. There are those who are striving for control aside from leadership. They will not contribute to the success of the leader. There are those who are eyeing the slot of leadership, inwardly hoping he will be a failure.

Those maneuvering for top slot do not realize the costs of leadership. On the surface it may look good, underneath it is lonely and painful. One older minister once said, "I'm lonely." More than 10 years ago I read, "Leadership is lonely"[1] Ten years later I now understand more fully the meaning of these three words.

One contributing factor to a leader's loneliness is the awareness that others would be as happy to see him fail as they would to see him succeed. They have failed to realize that making their leader successful will also make their own lives a success.

3. Learn to separate personality from the office.

If the policeman who stops you is rude, you may feel like giving him a piece of your mind. If he is kind, you may treat him with begrudging respect.

Is this proper? His office is to be respected, even if his personality is not the kindest. I agree, it is easier to respect a nice policeman than a rude one. However, God calls the Christian to respect the office of authority, even if the personality is not kind.

Paul was rudely treated by Ananias, the high priest. Paul replied in a similar manner in an attempt to set him straight. Others immediately asked him, "Revilest thou God's high priest?" (Acts 23:4).

"And Paul, earnestly beholding the council, said, Men and brethren, I have lived in all good conscience before God until this day. And the high priest Ananias commanded them that stood by him to smite him on the mouth. Then said Paul unto him, God shall smite thee, thou whited wall: for sittest thou to judge me after the law, and commandest me to be smitten contrary to the law? And they that stood by said, Revilest thou God's high priest? Then said Paul, I wist not, brethren, that he was the high priest: for it is written, Thou shalt not speak evil of the ruler of thy people" (Acts 23:1-5).

Paul's example indicates believers are to respect the office of authority in spite of the rudeness of those who hold it. People who fail to separate personality from leadership duties contribute to the loneliness of leadership. A leader must give direction in reaching decisions. He cannot direct decisions to please everyone's opinion. Those who are disappointed with the group's decision often aim their disappointment at the leader. They blame him directly for the congregation's decision. Some even bluntly tell him they feel betrayed, others gradually show a cold shoulder. Little by little, those who once were close friends start showing distance, and their personal relationship with their leader becomes strained. Their leader is left alone to ponder his inability to please everyone. Leadership can be a lonely place where relationships quickly become strained.

4. Use respectful titles.

The people who disrespectfully call their fathers "the old man" are encouraging disrespect for authority. The husband who calls his wife "the old lady" is feeding disrespect.

The worldly CB jargon about law enforcement officers does not implant respect. How can you respect a police officer if you call them anything but what is respectful? If we begin calling them "the fuzz," "the bears," "the big boys," or "the skullies," we are sowing seeds of disrespect.

Believers will do themselves a favor by weeding out all disrespectful terms from their vocabulary. When speaking of police officers, leaders, and people, use respectful terms; it encourages respect. The more respect you develop toward positions of authority, the better you will relate to authority.

What is your attitude toward authority? Have you submitted yourself to the scriptural teaching on authority? Does your attitude towards authority encourage others to be submissive? Does your attitude ultimately respect or disrespect the authority of God himself?

If your attitude and behavior toward authority is not scriptural, then do not expect to get along well with those around you. If it is not scriptural, then repent! Repent before the highest authority there is — God. Change your lifestyle so others will know you are respecting authority; and I assure you your relationships with others will be more rewarding.

Chapter 15

It Could Mean Suffering!

Who is the very best friend you have? The number one person in your life? The one you love with all your heart, strength, and soul? Who is that friend that sticketh closer than a brother? Jesus, of course!

We believers readily admit Jesus Christ is our best friend. If we are in trouble, we call on Him. When we are weak, we seek His strength. When we are depressed, we seek His presence. When we feel rejected, we have the assurance of His acceptance. When our believing loved ones die, we have hope.

In the midst of our hurts and sorrows, we identify with the man who wrote a poem to his mother with these words.

> What a Friend we have in Jesus,
> All our sins and griefs to bear;
> What a privilege to carry
> Everything to God in prayer.[1]

There is one word that describes the reason Jesus sticks closer than a brother. One word explains why He is our best friend. It is a quality we admire in Christ, but shrink from in our own lives. It is because of this one word that we can have our relationship with God restored. We love and appreciate this word when we see it demonstrated on our behalf in Jesus Christ. That word is suffering.

A widowed old grandfather has been close to his children during their growing years. His older years were crowned with beautiful grandchildren. Then as he is traveling the final stretch of his journey through life, he becomes painfully aware that a wall has risen between him and one of his children. He is heartbroken. He has done everything there is to do to try to remove the wall; yet the relationship has not improved. What can grandpa do?

Two sisters were very close to each other. They shared their joys, their sorrows, their fears, and concerns. They helped each other in their daily chores of life, and enjoyed social activities together. Then came a painful shock, as the one realized the other had withdrawn, and the good times were over. There was no explanation, no negotiation. A cold wall stood between them. Now what?

The marriage was beautiful. Everything looked so promising. They stood in front of their families and friends and vowed to God to be faithful in love until death takes one from the other. She was deeply committed to that vow. It was deeply rooted in her commitment of loyalty to God and the principles of His Word. Then her entire dream of the future crumbled as she learned that her husband was not faithful to his vow. He had been seen with another woman. She tried everything she knew to win his love back, but her only reward was a cold shoulder! What are her options?

There are people who are hurting because of strained relationships. They have examined their hearts to see if there is any hatred or jealousy. They have tried to keep the shock absorbers in place; they have solemnly expressed their feelings of rejection, and sought forgiveness. But nothing changes; they only continue in pain. What are their choices?

Could it be that this one word that was modeled for us by Jesus Christ is all that is left?

Let's go to the Upper Room where Jesus held the Passover with His disciples. Here we can see how Jesus responded to difficult and impossible people in His relationship.

"When Jesus had thus said, he was troubled in spirit, and testified, and said, Verily, verily, I say unto you, that one of you shall betray me. Then the disciples looked one on another, doubting of whom he spake. Now there was leaning on Jesus' bosom one of his disciples, whom Jesus loved. Simon Peter therefore beckoned to him, that he should ask who it should be of whom he spake. He then lying on Jesus' breast saith unto him, Lord, who is it? Jesus answered, He it is, to whom I shall give a sop, when I have dipped it. And when he had dipped the sop, he gave it to Judas Iscariot, the son of Simon. And after the sop Satan entered into him. Then said Jesus unto him, That thou doest, do quickly. Now no man at the table knew for what intent he spake this unto him. For some of them thought, because Judas had the bag, that Jesus had said unto him, Buy those things that we have need of against the feast; or, that he should give something to the poor. He then having received the sop went immediately out: and it was night" (John 13:21-30).

At this particular time, Jesus and His disciples are gathered around a table. One of those friends is going to betray Him. As they are preparing to eat, Jesus dips the bread and gives it to Judas, who is close to Him at the table. Judas is the first to receive food, a sign of honor. This is love's last appeal! Jesus is reaching out to him as a friend.[2]

In spite of Jesus' loving appeal to Judas, Satan entered into the heart of Judas that night. He left his friends, went out to the enemies of Jesus Christ, and betrayed Him for 30 pieces of silver. What was Christ's response to being totally betrayed by one of His close friends?

The path that Jesus took leads us to this one word that makes this relationship different from others. The option Jesus chose in that situation is the only response left for Christians in some relationships. From the writings of Peter we can clearly see what His unique response was.

"For Christ also hath once suffered for sins, the just for the unjust, that he might bring us to God, being put to death in the flesh, but quickened by the Spirit" (1 Pet. 3:18).

Jesus Christ took the road of suffering! We turned our backs to Him, we gave Him the cold shoulder, we spit into His face, we made fun of Him, we called Him names, we stripped Him of any dignity we could. And yet, His response was *suffering*.

He did not respond with retaliation. He did not try to even the score. He did not give us what we deserved. Rather, He suffered for us.

Why? To bring us back to God in a right relationship! Jesus took the path of suffering on behalf of good relationships. Sometimes suffering is the only option left other than breaking a relationship. Maintaining the relationship *could mean suffering!*

But who wants to suffer? That is part of our problem today. We are not willing to suffer for the sake of godly relationships. We are not willing to suffer for our own good, or for the benefit of the other person. Rather than suffering, we say, "I need more space." Wives leave notes on the kitchen table as they walk out of their husband's lives. Husbands claim they cannot stand their nagging wife. Teenagers run away from their parents, because they cannot stand living at home any more. People go from job to job, community to community, church to church, in search for a place where they will not have to suffer the annoyance of another's personality. The moving companies and U-Hauls are busy moving people away from each other. While there are legitimate reasons to move, there are times to suffer instead of running. In fact, Christians are to arm themselves for suffering.

"Forasmuch then as Christ hath suffered for us in the flesh, arm yourselves likewise with the same mind: for he that hath suffered in the flesh hath ceased from sin; That he no longer should live the rest of his time in the flesh to the lusts of men, but to the will of God" (1 Pet. 4:1-2).

Christ took the road of suffering for the sake of restoring relationships between God and man. The Bible instructs believers to follow Christ's example.

"For this is thankworthy, if a man for conscience toward God endure grief, suffering wrongfully. For what glory is it, if, when ye be buffeted for your faults, ye shall take it patiently? but if, when ye do well, and suffer for it, ye take it patiently, this is acceptable with God. For even hereunto were ye called: because Christ also suffered for us, leaving us an example, that ye should follow his steps: Who did no sin, neither was guile found in his mouth: Who, when he was reviled, reviled not again; when he suffered, he threatened not; but committed himself to him that judgeth righteously: Who his own self bare our sins in his own body on the tree, that we, being dead to sins, should live unto righteousness: by whose stripes ye were healed. For ye were as sheep going astray; but are now returned unto the Shepherd and Bishop of your souls" (1 Pet. 2:19-25).

Why should we suffer? Is there not a better way? Who loses if we run from suffering? Peter refers to a fiery trial which is to try you. Those painful trials and fiery ordeals will come. Our response will make us either bitter or better. If we become bitter, everyone involved loses. If we choose to allow these experiences to mellow us, it becomes a blessing to everyone.

What can we expect from suffering?

"Beloved, think it not strange concerning the fiery trial which is to try you, as though some strange thing happened unto you: But rejoice, inasmuch as ye are partakers of Christ's sufferings; that, when his glory shall be revealed, ye may be glad also with exceeding joy. If ye be reproached for the name of Christ, happy are ye; for the spirit of glory and of God resteth upon you: on their part he is evil spoken of, but on your part he is glorified. But let none of you suffer as a murderer, or as a thief, or as an evildoer, or as a busybody in other men's matters. Yet if any man suffer as a Christian, let him not be ashamed; but let him glorify God on this behalf. For the time is come that judgment must begin at the house of God: and if it first begin at us, what shall the end be of them that obey not the gospel of God? And if the righteous scarcely be saved, where shall the ungodly and the sinner appear? Wherefore let them that suffer according to the will of God commit the keeping of their souls to him in well doing, as unto a faithful Creator" (1 Pet. 4:12-19).

When trials come our way, what shall we look for?

1. A closer fellowship with Christ.

When everything goes as we wish, we tend to lose our focus on God. It is through suffering that we can more readily focus clearly on Christ's suffering. As we focus on Him, we partake of His suffering. As we fellowship with Him, we become like Him, and God's glory will be revealed in our lives to others.

2. *Becoming a temple of glory.*

Verse 14 tells us "for the spirit of glory and of God resteth upon you." When we seek to glorify God in our suffering, these trials can make us into a temple of glory.

When a relationship becomes strained, one of the first things we want is deliverance. We want the situation to change *now,* or we try to escape from its pressures. "I have just got to get away from this situation." "I must get away from my parents, I can't stand their nagging." "I have got to get away from the boss, or the co-worker who is causing all the trouble, or the wife who does not love me." We want deliverance, and we want it *now!*

It may be that God may not have deliverance in mind. God's ultimate plan for this particular situation may be development. As you run to escape, you may be running from God's plan for your life. God loves you dearly, and wants to see you develop for His glory. God may permit an irritable person to come into your life for the purpose of growth and maturity.

Larry Christenson made an excellent point. "We cry out, 'Lord, deliver me! What can I do to get out of this situation?' If *we listen,* the voice of God will say, 'I don't intend to get you out of it. I intend for you to go through it. The purpose for which this trouble has come is not that you be delivered, but that you be developed, that you become more like Jesus as you go through this experience.'"[3]

The lunch counter conversations that take place all over the country often end with the conclusion, "I've just got to get out of this situation." This may not be what God has in mind. You may be running away from God's plan for maturity and growth in your life.

3. *Receive its cleansing.*

Warren W. Wiersbe comments on 1 Peter 4:17-18: "Today, God is sending judgment to His church. In the Church there are both true believers and counterfeits. How does God separate the true from the false, the wheat from the chaff? He puts His church into the furnace, and the furnace becomes a crucible of cleansing. The dross appears, but the true believers are revealed the way they glorify God."[4]

When our relationships become strained, we tend to see the

faults of others. We then focus on changing the other person, or simply dropping our relationship with them. Again, that may not be what God has planned. He may have chosen that judgment and change is to begin with you. Maybe you are the house of God where judgment is to begin. Maybe you are the vessel where the dross or scum is to float to the top and be removed as you are melted with the baptism of fire.

The story is told of an experienced old blacksmith, who would sort through his metal. As he took pieces of metal in his experienced hand to examine it, some would be placed on one pile to be worked on later. As he glanced at other pieces, he would throw them on the junk heap.

A man who was watching asked, "Why is it that you throw some onto the junk heap and some over here?"

The blacksmith said, "I can see that some of the metal will be useful when it is put through the fire. There is something in it that will let it go through the fire and come out refined and perfected. But the other metal is useless. It cannot take the fire, so I have to toss it over onto the junk heap."[5]

When difficult times hit our relationships we often shrink back from the fire, and as a result we stumble into the junk heap. Much wiser is the man who cries, "Lord, the fire; not the junk heap!"

4. You can experience commitment.

The word translated commit is a banking term and refers to depositing money in the bank. This shows how valuable we are to God. We are His treasure, and He wants to protect us. It also shows us that we are safe in His hands. He purchased us, and He will guard us when we commit ourselves to Him.

When you put money in the bank, you expect to receive interest. When we put ourselves on the altar of dedication, God will give us spiritual dividends that will enrich our lives. We come out of the furnace richer than when we went in![6]

When we respond to suffering with a deeper commitment to

God, we can rest assured that God is at work. Our watchwords should be "Walk carefully, God is at work."

And finally, as you go through the fire of suffering, and misunderstanding, and simply not knowing why, I leave you with this story from Amy Carmicheal.

> The eternal substance of a thing never lies in the thing itself, but in the quality of our reaction toward it . . . and watch for the comforts of God. (In the midst of a sea battle) . . . when Earl Jellicoe was being misunderstood by the nation he served faithfully, a letter came from King George, whose keen sea sense had penetrated the mist which had bemused the general public. His letter heartened the fleet. What did anything matter now? *Their king knew.*
>
> Sometimes circumstances are so that we must be misunderstood, we cannot defend ourselves, we are open to blame, and yet we may know ourselves clear towards God and man in that particular matter. Then consider Him who endured, they laid to His charge things that He knew not.
>
> When you feel rejected, the King knows! When you have done all you could, and must suffer, the King knows![7]

When you have done all you know to do to heal the hurt and overcome the feelings of rejection, what options do you have? Could it be that suffering is your only option besides trying to run away from the problem? It may well be that running away will solve nothing, when God is working at developing your life and enriching your relationship with Him and others.

"Yea doubtless, and I count all things but loss for the excellency of the knowledge of Christ Jesus my Lord: for whom I have suffered the loss of all things, and do count them but dung, that I may win Christ, And be found in him, not having mine own righteousness, which is of the law, but that which is through the faith of Christ, the righteousness which is of God by faith: That I may know him, and the power of his resurrection, and the fellowship of his sufferings, being made conformable unto his death; If by any means I might attain unto the resurrection of the dead" (Phil. 3:8-11).

Think about this. A relationship without suffering is a relationship where the scum has not been cooked to the top for removal.

Suffering will bring rewards. For some it will be experienced in part here, and for others, the reward will wait until eternity, when God will wipe away all tears.

"But the God of all grace, who hath called us unto his eternal glory by Christ Jesus, after that ye have suffered a while, make you perfect, stablish, strengthen, settle you" (1 Pet. 5:10).

Chapter 16

Have a Friend, Be a Friend

Jesus was with His disciples in the Upper Room. He broke bread and ate with them. They all drank from one common cup. When the meal was over, Jesus stood up, took off His outer garment, and wrapped a towel around His waist. Then He poured water in a basin, and washed the feet of His disciples. As they spent the evening together, Jesus taught His disciples to love as He loved.

"This is my commandment, That ye love one another, as I have loved you. Greater love hath no man than this, that a man lay down his life for his friends. Ye are my friends, if ye do whatsoever I command you. Henceforth I call you not servants; for the servant knoweth not what his lord doeth: but I have called you friends; for all things that I have heard of my Father I have made known unto you. Ye have not chosen me, but I have chosen you, and ordained you, that ye should go and bring forth fruit, and that your fruit should remain: that whatsoever ye shall ask of the Father in my name, he may give it you. These things I command you, that ye love one another" (John 15:12-17).

After the teaching session, He led in His farewell prayer: "That they all may be one; as thou, Father, art in me, and I in thee, that they also may be one in us: that the world may believe that thou hast sent me. And the glory which thou gavest me I have given them; that they may be one, even as we are one" (John 17:21-22).

After the supper, the feet washing, the teaching, and the prayer, they sang a hymn together, and then went out to the Mount of Olives. Jesus knew He would soon be betrayed by one of His very own companions. He knew one of His friends would give a phony kiss of love that would deliver Him into the hands of sinful men armed with swords and clubs.

Jesus knew He would be led away to be tortured, beaten, scourged, mocked, and blasphemed. He knew that kiss of betrayal would ultimately lead Him to the cross of Calvary.

Jesus was facing the greatest test of His life. Notice something very significant in what Jesus said as He prayed in the garden. "And they came to a place which was named Gethsemane: and he saith to his disciples, Sit ye here, while I shall pray. And he taketh with him Peter and James and John, and began to be sore amazed, and to be very heavy; And saith unto them, My soul is exceeding sorrowful unto death: tarry ye here, and watch. And he went forward a little, and fell on the ground, and prayed that, if it were possible, the hour might pass from him. And he said, Abba, Father, all things are possible unto thee; take away this cup from me: nevertheless not what I will, but what thou wilt. And he cometh, and findeth them sleeping, and saith unto Peter, Simon, sleepest thou? couldest not thou watch one hour? Watch ye and pray, lest ye enter into temptation. The spirit truly is ready, but the flesh is weak. And again he went away, and prayed, and spake the same words. And when he returned, he found them asleep again, (for their eyes were heavy,) neither wist they what to answer him. And he cometh the third time, and saith unto them, Sleep on now, and take your rest: it is enough, the hour is come; behold, the Son of man is betrayed into the hands of sinners. Rise up, let us go; lo, he that betrayeth me is at hand" (Mark 14:32-42).

Here in Gethsemane, Jesus displayed a very basic human need of every heart and life. It is called *friendship!* Jesus had just told His disciples, "I have called you friends" (NAS). Now He faces the agonizing struggle before Calvary. "And he took with him Peter and James and John, and began to be very distressed and troubled. And He said to them, 'My soul is deeply grieved to the point of death; remain here and keep watch' " (Mark 14:33-34;NAS).

Jesus Christ, the Son of God, displayed a universal need that is in each of our lives. When we are in distress, we need friends! Everyone needs a close friend.

George was struggling with a sin. He could not live victoriously. He did not want to be a servant of sin, but he was stuck. Who could he turn to for help? He needs a trusted friend!

Mary Ann had been to her doctor. He had told her she and her husband could never bear children. Her heart was crushed as her dream of cuddling her own little baby was suddenly shattered. Her friends were mothers with happy families. She is deeply disappointed, hurt, and fighting jealousy toward her friends. What can she do, where can she go? She needs a friend.

Most of the fellows Ron's age are married. They happily bring their families to church activities and other social events. Ron is single. Every try at establishing a dating relationship has simply slipped away. He is depressed, thinks no one cares, and has considered suicide. He needs a friend!

"The world is filled with lonely people, and there are many Christians who find themselves in that position. We are surrounded by people we know, but not many of them could we consider genuinely close friends."[1]

Marie Chapman made an interesting point. "While most of us are busy pursuing romance and married love, our need for real friendship is often neglected. In some societies friendships are the most important relationship to be had."[2]

I believe she has a valid point. Romance and marital love has its place, but it also has its limits. Many believers do not get past its limits. They limit themselves jealously and possessively to their partner, and never experience the caliber of relationships with others that would enrich life for both of them. Their limitations deny them the experience that Solomon describes in Proverbs; "As iron sharpens iron, so one man sharpens another" (Prov. 27:17;NAS). Man was made for companionship. As steel whetted against a knife sharpens its edge, so can minds be strengthened and expanded as they share with each other.

Certainly, we have lots of friends, we smile at each other in church, then go home to be alone with our video games, stereos, and personal computers. These things cannot take the place of a close and caring friend with whom you can share.

The point is, we all have our personal Gethsemanes to a greater or lesser extent. We all need close friends to whom we can say, "Come with me, while I pray."

We find in the Scriptures that friendship played an important role in the lives of the men God used. Moses had Aaron and Joshua to support him. Daniel's remarkable life of faith was strengthened by his three friends. We discover in the Gospel of Mark that Jesus chose 12 to be with Him. There were three disciples with whom His relationship was closer, and with one, John, there was an added dimension of friendship and intimacy.

Paul constantly associated with friends. When he was in prison and facing death, he appealed to Timothy to come and bring him the books, and especially the parchments. He reminded Timothy that only Luke was with him, and that he should bring the cloak he left at Troas. (See 2 Tim. 4:9-13.) As Paul was facing his final Gethsemane, he, like Jesus, called for his friends to come to his side. These leaders of the faith displayed a universal need — they needed friends.

We all need friends, we all need a Peter, James, or John to listen to our tough times stories and encourage us. But, in order to have a friend, we must be a friend. Friendship is not handed to you on a silver platter. In order to have friends, we must be friends. To have a friend, you must be a friend. This is easier said than done. Friendships are very fragile and are easily broken. If they are left to follow their natural course, they soon evaporate.

Be a friend! Yes! But how? What are some basic guidelines of being a friend? The teaching of love that Jesus gave to His disciples before He laid down His life are the best set of instructions available to mankind. Let's look again at John 15:12-17. What is the key to friendship, and how do we cultivate it?

1. Love as Jesus loved (see verses 12-13).

The key to good healthy relationships is to "Love each other as I have loved you." Jesus had explained to the disciples that He loved them the way that His Father loved Him. Now, He said, they should pass that love on. "As the Father has loved me, so have I loved you . . ." (John 15:9;NIV).

How did He love His disciples? He loved them with a self-denying sacrificial love. This is the key to friendship — giving of yourself.

Jesus had not yet laid down His life for His disciples, but He reminded them, "No one has greater love — no one has shown stronger affection — than to lay down (give up) his own life for his friends" (John 15:13;AMP).

When we read this passage, we tend to think of literally dying. We think of crucifixion, of dying the way Jesus did. That may become the case. But I think it involves even more than literally dying. The Bible says, "And be ye kind one to another, tenderhearted, forgiving one another, even as God for Christ's sake hath forgiven you" (Eph. 4:32). Jesus made the point of laying down one's life for a friend before He himself died. As you observe His life up to this point, you will find it was filled with doing kind deeds. He reached out to troubled hearts, and made picnics for hungry stomachs. He rode a boat with His friends, and visited around the dinner table. After living a life of giving himself to others, He gave His life for us.

It is significant that the Bible says, "And let us consider how to stimulate one another to love and good deeds" (Heb. 10:24;NAS). The Living Bible states this as a challenging thought in relation to being a friend. "In response to all he has done for us, let us outdo each other in being helpful and kind to each other and in doing good."

Why should we outdo each other in doing good? Why are social activities important in expressing love in a relationship? Should we remember birthdays and anniversaries? Why the eating together and hospitality? Why does anyone need to go to such means in a relationship?

We have a van that has two gas tanks. If we are traveling and neglect to keep an eye on the fuel gauge of the regular tank, we are suddenly reminded by the sputtering and jerking of the engine that the tank is empty. We then flip a switch, and go on the reserve tank.

Relationships are similar. The regular tank, the daily grind, the rough side of the other person eventually gets to you, and you feel like giving up. That is when you need to switch to the reserve tank, and remember the steak dinner, the special treat, the trip to the park, and a dozen other kind and helpful deeds. It is in that spare tank that we store the reserves of assurances of love and acceptance. We all need that reserve tank to switch to at times.

2. *Love as He commanded* (see verse 14).

His command is that we love our neighbor as we love ourself. This kind of love gives in such a way that your friend will want to be a more faithful disciple of Jesus Christ because of your influence. You will give yourself in such a way that your friend will be encouraged to follow Jesus and obey His command of love. You will give yourself in such a way that will encourage your friend to become a closer friend of Jesus Christ.

3. *Love with His intimacy* (see verse 15).

Jesus was close and intimate with His disciples. He told them, "All I have heard from my Father I have made known unto you." People who become close friends are the ones who share their joys, sorrows, failures, and struggles with each other. They share in confession and seeking forgiveness.

Some people will *never* have close supporting friends. It is because they act as though they have their program all together, they grasp to be in control of the situation, and leave the impression they have very few sins. This attitude builds walls between this individual and those who are struggling with sin, and need a close friend. It is like Peter, James, and John falling asleep during Jesus' agony in Gethsemane.

4. *Love by His example* (see verse 16).

Jesus initiated the love and friendship He shared with people. This is exactly opposite of how many people respond. If others treat them nicely, they respond nicely in return. You were nice to me, so I will be nice to you. Jesus went beyond this love. "We love Him because He first loved us."

5. *Love by His goal* (see verse 17).

What is His goal for us? "That ye love one another."

Love your child, your friend, your spouse in such a way that he or she will want to follow you as you follow Christ, and also love one another. Love in a way to reproduce the Spirit fruit of love in others. Love in such a way to start a momentum of love rolling and growing. May the momentum roll out to the outside world where they can see the love of Christ demonstrated in us.

A Biblical Example

Do genuinely true friendships ever occur? David and Jonathan stand out again as an example and model, with lessons to be learned on how to be a friend. This friendship was forged between two men in the midst of great difficulties.

"God had knit those two potential enemies into a magnificent friendship that beautifully portrays essential features of a biblical friendship."[3]

Let's take another look at what they did that made them close friends. "And David abode in the wilderness in strong holds, and remained in a mountain in the wilderness of Ziph. And Saul sought him every day, but God delivered him not into his hand. And David saw that Saul was come out to seek his life: and David was in the wilderness of Ziph in a wood. And Jonathan Saul's son arose and went to David into the wood, and strengthened his hand in God. And he said unto him, Fear not: for the hand of Saul my father shall not find thee; and thou shalt be king over Israel, and I shall be next unto thee; and that also Saul my father knoweth" (1 Sam. 23:14-17).

The strengths of this relationship were largely a result of Jonathan's proper response to life.

1. Jonathan met David's need. Jonathan strengthened this friendship by being a friend when David needed him. David was fleeing for his life. King Saul, Jonathan's father, had determined to kill David. Jonathan rose up, and went to where David was suffering. He went to him, and gave him what he had — *himself.* He was a friend.

2. Jonathan encouraged David. He strengthened his hand in God. David was discouraged. He was a candidate for bitterness and resentment. Jonathan did not suggest to David that his problem was nothing to worry about. Neither did he act as though he had all the answers. He encouraged him in God by telling him that God had called him.

3. Jonathan shared in David's interest. He told him, "You shall be king over Israel." He affirmed God's call on David's life. He was not jealous, nor did he try to manipulate the position away from him. Jonathan was ready to help David realize God's purpose for his life. That is being a *friend*.

4. Jonathan and David declared loyalty and commitment. They made a covenant before the Lord (verse 18). They understood they were committed to true friendship. There is something freeing about being assured of friendship and loyalty from another. It allows me to freely function, and be myself. It assures me that you will not reject me. It affirms that I am of value to you.

There was a time when Choice Books of Northern Virginia was considering operating separately from the co-ordinating office in Harrisonburg, Virginia. The thought of parting felt threatening to both of us. We were under constant tension of indecision. Then we wrote and signed a three-year contract of working together. That felt good. We were both free to go on and do the work God called us to. That must have been the kind of thing David and Jonathan experienced.

What is a friend? Marie Chapin wrote, "A friend is someone I can call at hours of the day I would not call anyone else." "A friend is someone who sees me at my worst, but never forgets my best." "A friend is someone who I can be quiet with and who I can talk nonstop with."[4]

King Saul, Jonathan's father, did not have a good relationship with God or others. His sin of jealousy destroyed the relationship with David, and with his own son Jonathan.

Jonathan and David had a beautiful relationship. That is the kind of relationship to be treasured. But it will not be handed to you on a silver platter. If you want a loyal friend; you must be a loyal friend.

Be a friend! Have friends! It will help you over the rough spots in the journey through life. It will make the journey easier and more pleasant for everyone.

Chapter 17

Making Needed Changes

Haman had a serious problem!

However, he also had a lot of things going for him. He had vast holdings of wealth. If money could buy it, he probably had it. He was honored by having many sons. He had an elevated position with the king of the land and he had many friends!

Even with all these things, he still had a problem. The Scripture identifies the serious problem he was struggling with.

"Then went Haman forth that day joyful and with a glad heart: but when Haman saw Mordecai in the king's gate, that he stood not up, nor moved for him, he was full of indignation against Mordecai. Nevertheless Haman refrained himself: and when he came home, he sent and called for his friends, and Zeresh his wife. And Haman told them of the glory of his riches, and the multitude of his children, and all the things wherein the king had promoted him, and how he had advanced him above the princes and servants of the king. Haman said moreover, Yea, Esther the queen did let no man come in with the king unto the banquet that she had prepared but myself; and to morrow am I invited unto her also with the king. Yet all this availeth me nothing, so long as I see Mordecai the Jew sitting at the king's gate" (Esther 5:9-13).

"But all this gives me no satisfaction as long as I see that Jew Mordecai sitting at the king's gate" (NIV).

Haman's problem was a wrong attitude in the heart. This hateful attitude that was seated deep in his heart kept him from enjoying all those thing he possessed. It gave him no satisfaction. It meant nothing to him. He could not even be thankful for the blessings he had. He needed a change of heart. He definitely needed an attitude adjustment. More accurately, he needed a complete overhaul. Instead of making the needed changes, he concocted a plot to get rid of Mordecai. Instead of changing, he obeyed the natural instinct within him. Instead of changing and becoming a friend, he chose the route of separation by planning to kill Mordecai. Life would have been so much more pleasant for himself and everyone around him if he only would have changed.

Anthony Campolo relates a story that stands in sharp contrast to Haman. "A friend of mine tells the story of a mountaineer from West Virginia who fell in love with the beautiful daughter of the town preacher. The gruff and tough man one evening looked deeply into the eyes of the preacher's daughter and said, 'I love you.' It took more courage for him to say those simple words than he had to muster for anything else he had ever done. Minutes passed in silence, and then the preacher's daughter said, 'I love you, too.'

"The tough mountaineer said nothing except 'Good night.' Then he went home, got ready for bed and prayed, 'God, I ain't got nothin' against nobody.' "[1]

Do you notice the difference in one's life when someone says, "I love you," and the other answers, "I love you, too"? If only Haman would have changed his attitude, and chose love. He then could have enjoyed his wealth, his family, his job, and his friends.

In Genesis 42, we have an account of Jacob who was living during a time when there was a famine throughout the whole land. However, in Egypt, there was corn that was stored for the time of famine. Unknown to Jacob, his beloved son Joseph lived in Egypt, and was given the position next to Pharaoh. Twenty years earlier, Joseph had been sold by his brothers as a slave to merchant men. They had hated their brother, and could not speak a kind word to him.

As his brothers, Jacob's sons, came into Egypt to buy corn, they ran into problems, and ended up in jail. It was there that they said one to another, ". . . We are verily guilty concerning our brother, in that we saw the anguish of his soul, when he besought us, and we would not hear; therefore is this distress come upon us" (Gen. 42:21).

They still carried a guilty conscience from a wrong act 20 years earlier. Now everything in their lives revolved around Joseph. The person they "got rid of" is the one they really could not rid out of their minds. In a real way, Joseph controlled their actions and reactions. It was their attitude of hatred, envy, jealousy, and then guilt that controlled them.

That was not good enough for God. God wanted their lives changed. He wanted these brothers reconciled to each other. He wanted these brothers brought to the point where they embraced, wept aloud, and restored their relationship. The Bible says that Joseph ". . . kissed all his brethren, and wept upon them: and after that his brethren talked with him" (Gen. 45:15). In a later meeting, Joseph assured his brothers that he would provide for them and their little ones. He ". . . comforted them, and spake kindly unto them" (Gen. 50:21). These are the changes God wanted to see expressed in the lives of Jacob's sons.

As long as we are living, breathing human beings, God desires to see transformation in our lives. He wants to see our lives develop into the likeness of Jesus Christ. He asks us to bring even our thoughts under His lordship.

If the Holy Spirit has brought to your attention areas in your life that need changing, then respond to God, and co-operate with Him in making the needed changes. It will make life more enjoyable for you, and those around you.

Consider a few pointers that may suggest a need for change.

1. Tension means it needs attention.

If you have a broken thumb, you will give it priority attention. You will be careful how you handle it, and careful not to bump it. Tension in a relationship "sticks out like a sore thumb." It needs priority attention and care.

2. The "I really told him how it was" syndrome.

This is something that comes naturally. I used to think that the one who could tell the other "off" most skillfully was the winner. However; there are several serious problems with this approach. First, it provokes to anger. It pits anger against anger, and the wrath of man does *not* produce the righteousness of God in our lives. Secondly, seldom are you able to "tell it like it is." You may tell it as you perceive it to be, but that may not be the way the situation really is. The other individual has his point of view, his experience, and his side to tell. Telling him off misses the whole point. Thirdly, it is not speaking the truth in love. (See Eph. 4:15.) The Bible commands believers to speak the truth with love. You may lovingly tell a friend, "I feel rejected." That may be the truth. It expresses an emotional struggle you are battling with. It is not permissible to tell your friend, "You hate me." It may not be the truth, and is an attack on the other person's character. Lovingly express your emotional feelings and struggles, but never attack another's character.

There is a big difference! God may want you to do some soul-searching and changing.

3. The "you make me angry" guilt trip.

Some people use anger to control others. They tell others "You make me angry." Again, that is an attack on the other person, and it is not true. You do not make me angry, rather, I choose to become angry.

Depending on another's actions, I may feel emotions of anger and hurt. The truth is, I feel angry when you treat me that way. It is proper to lovingly and truthfully share your feelings. It is not loving or truthful to blame another for your outbursts of anger. While we are not to provoke another to anger, neither should it be necessary that everyone has to tip-toe around you, lest you become angry.

4. The controlling factor.

One of the natural traits we were born with is to break away, or walk off in a huff, if we cannot control the situation. If we do not get our way, we just drop the relationship. Cain did just that with his brother Abel, and became the world's first murderer. Haman tried to kill the person he could not control, and as a result, he lost his own life.

Believers use other methods. It is the cold shoulder, or the pickled tongue recipe. That was the method Joseph's brothers used against him before they sold him as a slave.

5. *Beware of trap doors!*

In Psalm 32, David identifies a common human problem of being trapped in silence about sins. In the first two verses he tells us what brings a blessing to our lives. "Blessed is he whose transgressions are forgiven, whose sins are covered. Blessed is the man whose sin the Lord does not count against him and in whose spirit is no deceit" (NIV).

In the third and fourth verses, he tells us what it is that causes him problems all day long. "When I kept silent, my bones wasted away through my groaning all day long. For day and night your hand was heavy upon me; my strength was sapped as in the heat of summer. Selah" (NIV).

In verse five he gives the answer to the problem. "Then I acknowledged my sin to you and did not cover up my iniquity. I said, 'I will confess my transgressions to the Lord' — and you forgave the guilt of my sin. Selah" (NIV).

Here are some applications. When you keep silent about an inner struggle, it saps you of strength and joy. Bitterness can cause inner groanings all day long. A common problem we encounter is that we want to hide and bury our struggles with sins of the heart. If we keep silent, they will cause us to waste away.

You have friends to share with. God may want you to share your struggles with a close friend who will stand with you and encourage you to make needed changes. Prolonged silence about your inner struggles, fears, and pains is not good for your relationship with God or others.

6. *Beware of closed ears.*

It is possible that there are deaf spots in your hearing habits. Are people trying to nicely suggest that you have ways that tend to hurt and insult others?

Some of your ways and conduct may be like bad breath — very offensive and painful to those close to you. We may not be aware of the discomfort we cause others, and do not understand why others run away from us. When someone is trying to bring to your attention your weaknesses, listen closely for clues of hurt. God may open areas to you that He wants changed in your life.

Old habits and lifestyles are hard to change. We tend to run along the well-worn groove we have established. To start a new path is difficult.

For about 10 years I was accustomed to reaching for the light switch for the hallway on the left side of my study door. After our house was gutted with fire, the location of the switch was changed in the rebuilding. It took years of reprogramming to change the location of the switch in my mind. In fact, I must at times yet make a conscious effort to find the switch.

Sinful and negative habits we have are hard to change. They become stuck in our lives like alcohol to an alcoholic. To really change will require intense effort, determination, and retraining of habits.

Pastor Earl V. Karl told me of an experience he went through that illustrates this point. He was wounded in the Vietnam War, and a nerve was damaged in his arm. He lost control of the movement of one hand, wrist, and fingers. He could not raise the wrist or fingers. He went through a series of operations at the Bethesda Naval Hospital. Following these operations, he was required to go through very intense therapy to retrain the brain to send signals to the wrist and fingers. It took six months of training for the middle finger to make movements. The training consisted of consciously thinking and telling the fingers and hand what to do. If he wanted to turn a page in the Bible, he had to stop and send a signal from the brain to the hand and tell it what to do. Finally, five years later, he could unconsciously use his hand again.

Retraining and reprogramming takes intense effort. You must be serious about it if you want changes to take place. The benediction in Hebrews is so appropriate. "Now the God of peace, that brought again from the dead our Lord Jesus, that great shepherd of the sheep, through the blood of the everlasting covenant, Make you perfect in every good work to do his will, working in you that which is wellpleasing in his sight, through Jesus Christ; to whom be glory for ever and ever. Amen" (Heb. 13:20-21).

Changes can happen as we cooperate with the Master Therapist, respond to His instructions, and allow the Holy Spirit to reshape our thoughts and ways.

When a traveler boards an airliner for a journey, he is welcomed on board by a flight attendant. He is given instructions on what to do for safety and comfort. They will thank him for flying with their airline, and wish each passenger a pleasant trip. After they are airborne, they serve their passengers something to eat and drink. The pilot may choose to announce how high they are flying, the weather conditions at the destination, and the expected arrival time. He also assures them of a safe journey.

Life is a journey! It is a trip from birth into eternity. The habits of life we follow can make it a pleasant trip or a trauma; both for yourself and those traveling with you. May you experience God's grace in applying oil to your relationships rather than sand that destroys. God grant you smooth traveling, and a safe landing in His presence.

Self Test on Desirable Traits in our Relationships

E - Excellent, G - Good, L - Livable, N - Needs Improvement

   Relating to strangers _____
   Getting along with others:
      socially _____
      church level _____
      with those close to me _____
      with my family _____
      applying oil instead of sand _____
      conquering natural responses _____
      responding biblically _____
      practicing Holy Limp and Holy Lips _____
      strenuous effort to show love to others _____
   Victorious over the sins of the heart:
      jealousy _____
      envy _____
      selfishness _____
      pride _____
   Keeping shock absorbers in place _____
   Solemnly reproving when needed _____
   Restoration as a goal in reproving _____
   Responding well when corrected _____

Confessing wrongs to others _____

Seeking forgiveness and restoration _____

Ability to be non-defensive _____

Renouncing destructive habits through
    repentance _____

Extending forgiveness that restores closeness _____

Forgiving without continued grudges _____

Functioning well in groups _____

Laying down the ME ambition _____

Blending well into WE projects _____

Practice of accountability _____

Accountable to those close to you _____

Working well with others _____

Ability to work without being in control _____

Attitude toward employer/employees _____

Showing respect for authority _____

Working at making others successful _____

Willingness to suffer when mistreated _____

Suffering rather than breaking the relationship _____

Ability to be a close friend _____

Loving as Jesus loved _____

Giving encouragement to others _____

Making the needed changes _____

Endnotes

Chapter 1
[1]Gary Inrig, *Quality Friendships* (Chicago, IL: Moody Press, 1981), p. 97.

Chapter 2
[1]Inrig, *Quality Friendships,* p. 17.

Chapter 3
[1]Dale E. Galloway, *You Can Win With Love* (Irvine, CA: Harvest House, 1976).

[2]Harry Verploegh, editor, *Oswald Chambers, The Best from all His Books* (Nashville, TN: Thomas Nelson Publishers, 1987), p. 314.

[3]*Confident Living,* September 1987, p.51.

[4]R. C. Sproul, *The Holiness of God* (Wheaton, IL: Tyndale House Publishers, 1985).

[5]James Holt, *How to Have a Better Relationship with Anybody* (Chicago, IL: Moody Press, 1984).

Chapter 4
[1]Information from *Straight Talk From Marmaduke About Canine Heartworm Disease* (Norden Laboratories, Inc., Lincoln, NE, 1979).

[2]Sproul, *The Holiness of God.*

Chapter 5
[1]Jerry Johnson, *Why Suicide* (Nashville, TN: Oliver-Nelson Books, 1987).

[2]Galloway, *You Can Win with Love.*

[3]Paul E. Billheimer, *Love Covers* (Minneapolis, MN: Bethany House Publishers, 1981).

[4]Allan Loy McGinnis, *The Friendship Factor* (Minneapolis, MN: Augsburg Publishing House, 1979).

[5]Vance Havner, *The Vance Havner Quotebook* (Grand Rapids, MI: Baker Book House, 1986).

[6]John L. DeLorean with Ted Schwartz, *DeLorean* (Grand Rapids, MI: Zondervan Publishing House, 1985), p.59.

[7]Don Baker, *A Fresh New Look at God* (Portland, OR: Multnomah Press, 1987).

Chapter 6
[1]Richard P. Walters, *How to Be a Friend* (Ventura, CA: Regal Books, 1981).

[2]Richard P. Walters, *The Weed of Greed* (Grand Rapids, MI: Zondervan Publishing House, 1985).

[3]Walters, *How to Be a Friend.*

[4]Anthony Campolo, *Seven Deadly Sins* (Wheaton, IL: Victor Books, 1987), p. 92.

[5]Ibid.

[6]Inrig, *Quality Friendships.*

[7]C.S. Lewis, Mere Christianity (New York, NY: MacMillan Publishing Co., 1943), p. 116.

[8]Campolo, *Seven Deadly Sins*, p.25.

[9]*Prison Ministry Newsletter,* Nov/Dec 1987.

Chapter 7

[1]Richard Strauss, *Getting Along with Each Other* (San Bernardino, CA: Here's Life Publishers, 1985), p.52.

[2]Jay Adams, *Handbook of Church Discipline* (Grand Rapids, MI: Zondervan Publishing House, 1986).

[3]Carolyn Beachey, *Brotherhood Beacon,* Jan. 1988.

Chapter 8

[1]Strauss, *Getting Along with Each Other,* p. 28.

[2]Strauss, *Getting Along with Each Other.*

[3]Ibid.

[4]Inrig, *Quality Friendships.*

[5]William Backus, *Telling Each Other the Truth* (Minneapolis, MN: Bethany House Publishers, 1985), p. 22-23.

[6]Inrig, *Quality Friendships.*

[7]Strauss, *Getting Along with Each Other.*

[8]James Hilt, *How to Have a Better Relationship with Anybody* (Chicago, IL: Moody Press, 1984), p. 64-65.

[9]John Edward Jones, *Reconciliation* (Minneapolis, MN: Bethany House Publishers, 1984), p. 149.

Chapter 9

[1]David Augsburger, *Caring Enough to Confront* (Scottdale, PA: Herald Press, 1973).

[2]Ken Wilson, *How to Repair the Wrongs You've Done* (Ann Arbor, MI: Servant Publications, 1982), p. 13.

[3]Dr. Paul Faulkner, *Making Things Right* (Fort Worth, TX: Sweet Publishing, 1986), p. 50.

[4]John M. Drakeford, *The Awesome Power of the Listening Ear* (Grand Rapids, MI: Zondervan Publishing House, 1982), p. 113.

[5]Ray Stedman, *Body Life* (Ventura, CA: Regal Books, 1972), p. 113.

[6]McGinnis, *The Friendship Factor,* p. 111.

[7]Strauss, *Getting Along with Each Other,* p. 151.

[8]Vance Havner, *Playing Marbles with Diamonds* (Grand Rapids, MI: Baker Book House, 1985), p. 59.

[9]Wilson, *How to Repair the Wrongs You've Done,* p. 23.

[10]Ibid.

[11]Ibid.

[12]Ibid.

[13]Ibid.

[14]Ibid.

[15]Dr. Faulkner, *Making Things Right.*

Chapter 10

[1]Dorris Donnelly, *Learning to Forgive* (Nashville, TN: Abingdon Press, 1989), p. 74.

[2]Roger L. Fredrikson, *The Commentator's Commentary, John* (Waco, TX: Word Books, 1985), p. 224.

[3]Simon Schrock, *One-Anothering* (Green Forest, AR: New Leaf Press, 1991), p. 63.

[4]Ibid.

[5]McGinnis, *The Friendship Factor*, p. 157.

[6]Faulkner, *Making Things Right*, p. 119.

[7]Myron Augsburger, *The Commentator's Commentary, Matthew* (Waco, TX: Word Books, 1982).

[8]Verplough, *Oswald Chambers, The Best from All His Books.*

[9]Tim Lahaye, *Anger Is a Choice* (Grand Rapids, MI: Zondervan Publishing House, 1982), p. 51.

[10]Dwight L. Carlson, *Overcoming Hurts and Anger* (Irvine, CA: Harvest House Publishers, 1981), p. 180.

[11]Doris Donnelly, *Learning to Forgive* (Nashville, TN: Abingdon Press, 1989), p. 32.

[12]Simon Schrock, *Get On with Living* (Green Forest, AR: New Leaf Press, 1993), p. 69.

[13]Simon Schrock, *The Price of Missing Life* (Green Forest, AR: New Leaf Press, 1981), p. 94-95.

[14]Richard P. Walters, *Forgive and Be Free* (Grand Rapids, MI: Zondervan Publishing House, 1983), p. 117-118.

[15]Wilson, *How to Repair the Wrongs You've Done*, p. 52.

[16]Ibid.

[17]McGinnis, *The Friendship Factor*, p. 160-161.

[18]James C. Halley, *Searchlight on Bible Word* (Grand Rapids, MI: Zondervan Publishing House, 1972), p. 121, quoted from LaHaye, *Anger Is a Choice*, p. 31.

Chapter 11

[1]*The World Book Encyclopedia*, 1984.

[2]Ralph Earle, *Word Meanings in the New Testament* (Grand Rapids, MI: Baker Book House), p. 318.

[3]Richard Halverson, *Walk with God Between Sundays* (Palm Springs, CA: Roynald Haynes Publishers, 1981).

[4]*The Washington Post*, November 10,1988.

[5]Halverson, *Walk with God Between Sundays.*

Chapter 12

[1]*The Washington Post*, February 25, 1988.

[2]Henry Morris, *The Genesis Record* (Grand Rapids, MI: Baker Book House, 1976), p. 116.

[3]Morris, *The Genesis Record.*

[4]*Mennonite Brethren Herald,* Jim Coggins, editor, December 9, 1988, p. 12.

[5]Ted Engstrom, *Your Leadership Skills* (Nashville, TN: Power Sound Cassette, Thomas Nelson Inc.).

[6]Ted Engstrom, *The Making of a Christian Leader* (Grand Rapids, MI: Zondervan Publishing House, 1976), p. 206.

[7]*The Christian Leadership Letter,* November 1987.

[8]Strauss, *Getting Along with Each Other,* p. 70-71.

[9]Charles Bridges, *Modern Studies in the Book of Proverbs* (Milford, MI: Molt Media, 1978).

[10]*Christian Leadership Letter,* November 1987.

[11]J. Carl Laney, *A Guide to Church Discipline* (Minneapolis, MN: Bethany House Publishers), p. 161.

Chapter 13

[1]Jerry and Mary White, *Your Job, Survival or Satisfaction* (Grand Rapids, MI: Zondervan Publishing House, 1977).

[2]*The Washington Post,* November 20, 1986.

[3]*Topical Encyclopedia of Famous Quotations* (Minneapolis, MN: Bethany House Publishers, 1982), p. 259.

[4]Verplough, *Oswald Chambers, The Best from All His Books.*

[5]White, *Your Job, Survival or Satisfaction,* p. 30.

Chapter 14

[1]Engstrom, *The Making of a Christian Leader,* p. 85.

Chapter 15

[1]Joseph Scriven, "What a Friend We Have in Jesus."

[2]Fredrickson, *The Commentators Commentary, John,* p. 224.

[3]Larry Christenson, *The Renewed Mind* (Minneapolis, MN: Bethany Fellowship, 1974), p. 106.

[4]Warren Wiersbe, "Glorifying God," *Good News Broadcaster* (Lincoln, NE: Back to the Bible), p. 29.

[5]Christenson, *The Renewed Mind.*

[6]Wiersbe, *Glorifying God.*

[7]Amy Carmichael, *Growing through Rejection* (Wheaton, IL: Tyndale House Publishers, 1983), p. 44.

Chapter 16

[1]Inrig, *Quality Friendships,* p. 15.

[2]Marie Chapman, *Growing Closer* (Old Tappan, NJ: Fleming H. Revell Co., 1986), p. 39.

[3]Inrig, *Quality Friendships,* p. 24.

[4]Chapman, *Growing Closer.*

Chapter 17

[1]Campolo, *Seven Deadly Sins.*

You may contact Simon Schrock
through

Choice Books
11923 Lee Highway
Fairfax, VA 22030
(703) 830-2800